Super Science Themes

Written by
Elizabeth Kelly and Joanne McConville

Cover Design by
Jannette Bole and Matthew Van Zomeren

Inside Illustrations by
Becky Radtke

Published by Instructional Fair • TS Denison
an imprint of

McGraw-Hill
Children's Publishing

About the Authors
In addition to her classroom experiences in elementary and art education, Elizabeth Kelly has been a member of Hathaway Brown School's early childhood department for many years. In that role, she and Joanne McConville helped to develop and successfully launch the three-year-old program. Both women are committed to providing new and interesting learning experiences for young children.

With degrees in elementary education and special education, Joanne McConville has taught both developmentally delayed and kindergarten children. At the present time she teaches preschool.

This is the third book that Ms. Kelly and Ms. McConville have co-authored for McGraw-Hill Children's Publishing. Their previous two books, *Young Minds at Play* and *Art for the Very Young*, have both won the Director's Choice Award.

Acknowledgments
Many thanks to Jane Brown (and her dog Francis), science consultant and director of Early Childhood at Hathaway Brown School, for her generous and gracious help, inspiration, and guidance.

Credits
Authors: Elizabeth Kelly and Joanne McConville
Cover Design: Jannette Bole, Matthew Van Zomeren
Inside Illustrations: Becky Radtke
Project Director/Editor: Debra Olson Pressnall
Editors: Mary Rose Hassinger, Sara Bierling
Graphic Design and Layout: Jannette Bole
Cover Photos: Artville, PhotoDisc

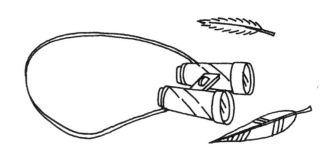

McGraw-Hill Children's Publishing
A Division of The **McGraw-Hill** Companies

Published by Instructional Fair • TS Denison
An imprint of McGraw-Hill Children's Publishing
Copyright © 2002 McGraw-Hill Children's Publishing

Send all inquiries to:
McGraw-Hill Children's Publishing
3195 Wilson Drive NW
Grand Rapids, Michigan 49544

Super Science Themes
ISBN: 0-7424-0247-9

1 2 3 4 5 6 7 8 9 07 06 05 04 03 02

Table of Contents

How to Use This Book

Young children are naturally drawn to stories. *Super Science Themes* integrates this interest in stories with the study of animals. Opportunities to manipulate and observe items on the science table, lively activities that incorporate the five senses, and kinesthetic experiences to reinforce key concepts—these components are all present within the themes. Essential skills for both language arts and science curricula are also integrated in the animal themes as children are provided opportunities for observing, describing, recording, predicting, inferring, and communicating.

 **Stories**

Each unit begins with a story about a dog's adventure with nature. The stories combine the fiction of the dog's adventures with factual information about a variety of animals. The children will identify with the dog in the stories and anticipate his adventures while they look forward to the accompanying learning experiences. Draw the children into the story by showing them a picture of Russell (page 128). If appropriate, take some time to talk with the children about pets. Ask the children to point out something about Russell that they like. Would they like a pet like Russell? Why or why not? What other kinds of pets do they like?

The stories are only a framework for you to use. Before sharing a story with the children, read through it carefully and think about how you would explain the particular events. It is important to feel comfortable with the story and to tell it in your own words. Bring the picture of the dog to every story time. It will help to draw the children into the story and the subject matter and will serve as an aid in retention. Also bring a photocopy of the animal pattern page that is provided for each

theme or several full-color pictures of the animal from books or magazines. One or two other items listed for the Interactive Display should also be brought to story time. Reveal the items at the end of the story.

Each story incorporates the traditional participation technique of rhythmic tapping and body motions that the children will delight in doing along with you. To hold the group's interest, the children are also encouraged to imitate various sounds that are part of the story. Do not be afraid to stop mid-story for comments and/or audience participation.

For the youngest learners, it may be appropriate to tell the story, introduce an item or two from the Interactive Display, and then send home a Take Home Bag with each child. During the following week, do a finger play at circle time, play a game, and have the children complete one of the activities.

 **Interactive Display**

The Interactive Display is an essential component of the program because it offers sensory experiences that make learning more viable. Introduce any items that are not self-explanatory but also encourage the children to explore and experiment on their own. Prepare the science table by displaying various objects that have been collected.

Although there are several ideas for each science table, building up such a complete Interactive Display will take a considerable length of time. Start off with a few items that are easily obtainable and appropriate. Add some new items each time you use the unit. Teachers of very young children may want to keep their Interactive Display quite simple. A good rule of thumb is, the younger the child, the simpler the display.

The Internet and old calendars are good and inexpensive sources for animal pictures. Other possible sources for information and/or field trips include: local museums, zoos, nature stores, sporting goods stores, State Department of Natural Resources, local game and fish wardens, taxidermists, parks, park rangers, pet shops, pet owners, yard sales, antique dealers/collectors, hunters, fishermen, and sport or camping enthusiasts.

Take Home Bag

The Take Home Bag is a vital part of the program because it serves as a liaison between school and home. The pictures and the "Fun Facts" are essential components. The picture of Russell will help children recall the story as they tell about Russell's adventures at home. The Fun Facts will provide a springboard for conversation between parent and child. The other suggested items that are listed for each Take Home Bag are optional. Include them at your discretion.

Fun Facts

The contents of the Fun Facts sheet speak to the natural curiosity that children have about topics in nature and are designed with an age span in mind. The "Fun Facts" can be copied for the Take

Home Bag. The youngest learners may be ready for only a few facts, while older children will be ready for several more. Share only the facts that you feel are appropriate for your group.

Activities

The activities are designed to reach the youngest learner and to extend to meet the needs of older children. There are a wide variety of experiences including math, games, movement, drama, finger plays, and art. You may choose to do a science-related activity each day or choose just one as an introduction or culmination activity. Included are ideas for integrating each unit with other topics.

To make an animal puzzle for each theme, photocopy the animal pattern page. Color and mount it onto poster board. Cut the picture into puzzle pieces and then laminate them for durability. Allow the children opportunities to assemble the pieces to show the animal's picture.

Parent Meeting Note:
If you decide to use several of these units in your program, you may find it helpful to discuss the animal themes with your parents at one of your parent meetings. Alert them to look for the Take Home Bag and encourage them to talk with their children about its contents.

Introducing Ants

What child has not seen ants at a picnic, in the house, or outdoors while playing? Oftentimes, the first reaction is to step on the ants. Many young children regard them simply as pests. However, ants are hard-working insects, strong beyond belief, and members of nature's clean-up crew.

Suggested Visuals

- Picture of Russell
- Pictures of ants from books and/or the Internet
- Rubber/plastic models of ants
- A backpack filled with picnic treats, such as dog biscuits, an apple, and a package of crackers
- One or two large blankets

 ## Telling the Story

Spread the blanket(s) on the floor and gather your students together for a story time. Bring your choice of items from the display area but keep them covered. Show the children a picture of Russell. Tell the following story in your own words.

Sometimes Russell and I take a backpack full of treats on our walks in the woods. We like to spread out a blanket and eat our treats under a shady tree. Here is my backpack. Would you like to see what I brought? (*Pull out the items one by one to share. Pass the crackers around for the children to snack on while you continue.*) Russell gets very excited when he sees me packing my backpack because he loves to go on picnics.

(*Ask the children if they have ever gone on picnics. Take some time to listen to their comments.*) Russell was so excited about the picnic that he was walking his very fastest walk. (*Pat hands on thighs quickly.*) I was walking a slower walk, like this. (*Tap hands on thighs slowly.*) Russell was up ahead of me, headed for our special picnic place. He began to run. (*Start a running rhythm.*) I kept on walking (*Pat a walking rhythm on thighs.*) because I knew that Russell would stop and wait for me once he reached the shady trees where we always stop to eat. When I arrived, Russell was waiting for his treats. I quickly spread out the blanket and offered Russell his treats while I ate mine. After we ate, we rested. I was resting on my back, looking at the clouds. Russell was sniffing around the blanket, looking for any crumbs that we had left behind. Suddenly, he began to growl, deep in his throat. It sounded like this. Groooowwwwwwl. (*Make a deep growling sound. Ask the children to make the sound, too.*) That sound means that Russell is very angry. I turned to see what the problem was. There was Russell, crouched down, watching some of his delicious crumbs walking off the blanket. I said, "Hustle, Russell. We need to go to the library to find out what kind of creature walks off with crumbs."

Discussing the Story

Ask the children if they know what animal might walk off with Russell's crumbs. Make a list of their ideas. Introduce the pictures and/or models of ants to the children, saying, "Here are the animals that were taking Russell's crumbs. What are they called?" After the students answer, ask them to share some of their experiences with ants. Where have they seen ants? What were the ants doing?

As the children continue to look at the materials you have collected, share some interesting facts about ants from the "Fun Facts to Share" sheet. Invite the children to ask questions. If you cannot answer their questions, look the answers up together. Older students will be ready for longer and more detailed explanations and to look up information on their own.

Integrating This Unit

- Try setting up a patio or deck in your dramatic play area. Use large unit blocks for flooring. Provide a table and chairs, a clip-on umbrella, plastic dishes, a play grill, flower boxes/pots, gardening tools, and artificial flowers. Have several "picnics" in this area while talking about ants.

- Ants and honeybees have much in common. While your deck/patio is in place, explore the topic of honeybees after the unit on ants is finished. Encourage your group to compare and contrast the two species.

Interactive Display for Ants

Choose from the following:
- Picture of Russell
- Several pictures of various kinds of ants
- Rubber or plastic models of ants
- A model or drawing of the life cycle of the ant
- Live display:
    1. Fill a large jar half-full with soil and add some leaves.
    2. Place some seeds on a piece of cardboard (outdoors) to attract some garden ants.
    3. Drop the ants in the jar.
    4. Add a small damp sponge for a water source.
    5. Punch some holes in the jar lid for air.
    6. Keep the jar in a dark place until you want to watch the ants.
    7. Let the ants go free outdoors when you are done observing them.
- Fiction and nonfiction books about ants

Take Home Bag for Ants

Place one or more of the following items in each child's resealable plastic bag. Send the bag home following the introduction or at the end of the unit.

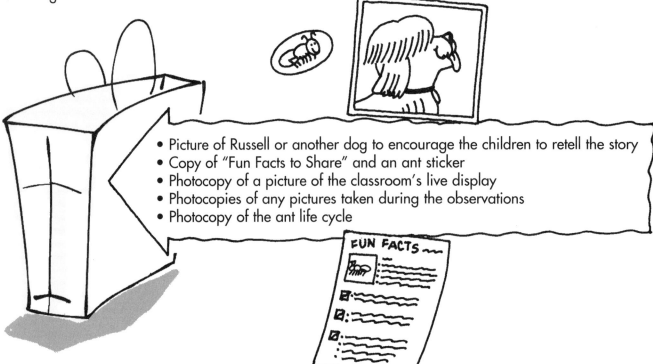

- Picture of Russell or another dog to encourage the children to retell the story
- Copy of "Fun Facts to Share" and an ant sticker
- Photocopy of a picture of the classroom's live display
- Photocopies of any pictures taken during the observations
- Photocopy of the ant life cycle

FUN FACTS to Share

ant

About Its Body
- The ant's body has three main parts—the head, thorax, and abdomen.
- Its body has a hard shell-like covering.
- On its head are antennae. The ant uses them for tasting, smelling, hearing, and touching.
- In its abdomen are two stomachs. One is for its own food. The other stores food for other ants.
- Ants are very strong. They can carry an object that is 10 times their body weight.

Food
- Some ants feed on caterpillars, flies, beetles, and the sugar drops from aphids.

Habitat
- The nest is dark with many rooms and tunnels. Each room has a special purpose, such as resting spot, pantry, and nursery. During a cold winter, the ants sleep in a room near the bottom of the nest.
- An ant has many enemies. Some are frogs, birds, anteaters, lizards, spiders, and toads.

Habits
- Ants are social insects. They live together in colonies where each has a job. The queen is the largest ant. Her job is to lay eggs while others care for her. The workers are nurses, food gatherers, soldiers, farmers, and builders.
- Many ants have a dumping ground outside the nest where they bury trash.
- Ants groom themselves and each other.
- Ants put down a scent trail to find their way back to their home and to direct other ants to food.

Activities for Ants

- Observe ants and write or record the children's observations in a class book. Older children may write and illustrate their own observation books.

  You will need:
  the live display, magnifying glasses, and several large sheets of lined paper for recording the students' observations (small individual notebooks for older students). If possible, take pictures to help illustrate the book(s).

  1. While the ants are in the jar, add some bread crumbs. Have the students observe the ants through a magnifying glass. Record their observations.
  2. Add a couple of drops of water and see how the ants act. Record the students' observations.
  3. Place the ant jar in the refrigerator for 20 minutes (the cold will slow the ants down). Record the students' observations.
  4. Place the jar in a pan of water so the ants cannot escape. Remove the lid from the jar and cover the top with a piece of plywood with a hole cut in it. Place the hole over the opening in the jar. Put a small piece of bark with honey on it on top of the plywood. Cover the entire display with a box, as the ants do not care for too much light. Remove the box in a couple of days and see what has happened. Record the students' observations.
  5. Locate an anthill. Weather permitting, take your group outside to observe ant life. Fill several small flat containers with different kinds of food (bread crumbs, honey, sugar, flour). Place the containers in a circle about three feet from the anthill. Notice which foods the ants like best, how long it takes the ants to find the food, and how the ants travel to the food. Record observations.

- Cut an anthill shape from a piece of brown butcher paper. Draw a series of tunnels and rooms on the anthill shape. Share information about anthills. Label each room according to its purpose. Have your students add the ants to the nest by providing them with pencil erasers, felt-tip pens, and ink pads. Instruct the children to print three connecting dots for the ant's body using the erasers and ink pads, then add six legs to the bodies using the markers. Hang the "anthill" on a wall near your display area.

- Construct an ant nest in your room with boxes. Acquire several (4–6) boxes from parents, local businesses, neighbors, etc. that are large enough to allow your students to crawl and/or sit. Arrange the boxes to provide your students with a series of tunnels and rooms. Have each student choose an "ant job" and bring something from the classroom or from home to the nest that illustrates that job, such as seeds, baby care items, or grooming items.

- Read aloud the book "I Can't" Said the Ant by Polly Cameron (Scholastic Books, 1963) to your class. If necessary, discuss rhyming words. Encourage the class to make up simple rhymes about ants. Write their ideas on a large sheet of chart paper. Have the group continue to create rhymes about other insects. Each rhyme will become a page in a class rhyming book about insects. Photocopy the book and give each child a copy to illustrate and take home in his/her Take Home Bag.

- Perform the finger play:
    Lots of insects have time to rest, (*Rest head on hands, palms together.*)
    But ants are busy in their nest. (*Link fingers, palms up, and wiggle fingers.*)
    Monkeys play—just like you, (*Scratch your sides like a monkey.*)
    But worker ants have lots to do. (*Link fingers, palms up, and wiggle fingers.*)
    Birds build nests up in the trees, (*Fold arms like wings and flap.*)
    But ants live in a colony. (*Link fingers, palms up, and wiggle fingers.*)
    It's hard to see a deer in the sun, (*Circle eyes with fingers to mimic glasses.*)
    But watching ants is lots of fun! (*Link fingers, palms up, and wiggle fingers.*)

- Demonstrate the great strength of ants. Bring 11 unit blocks with you to group time. Pass one of the blocks around and ask the children to pretend that this is the size and weight of one ant. Now make a stack with the other 10 blocks. Have the children count the blocks as you stack them. Explain that this is how many blocks an ant this size (*hold up single block*) could lift and carry. Have the students take turns lifting the stack. Show the children some pictures of things that are approximately ten times their weight, such as ten of their classmates, four or five adults, a small pony, a motor scooter, etc. Would they be able to lift any of these things?

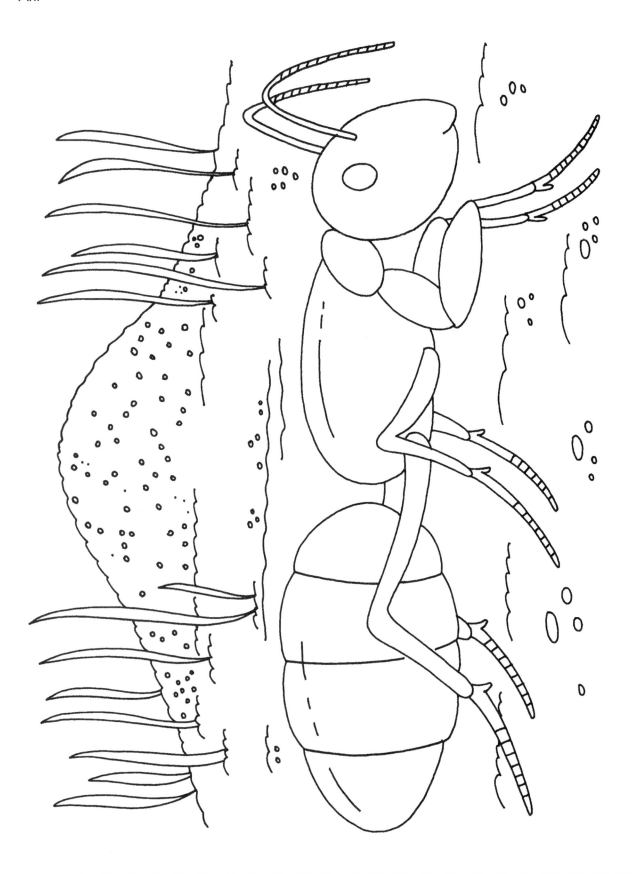

queen

worker

eggs

larvae

pupa

pupa (inside view)

Introducing Earthworms

Children are always surprised and delighted to find paved surfaces covered with earthworms after a heavy rain shower. They find the temptation to touch them almost irresistible. Whether worms provoke a squeamish or curious response, earthworms are creatures that young children want to know about.

Suggested Visuals

- Picture of Russell
- Pictures of earthworms in books
- Plastic worms from a sporting goods or discount store
- Chewy worm-shaped candies, one per child

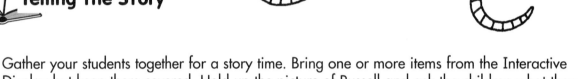

 **Telling the Story**

Gather your students together for a story time. Bring one or more items from the Interactive Display but keep them covered. Hold up the picture of Russell and ask the children what they remember about Russell. Tell this story in your own words.

My dog Russell is a great detective. He is also a hero. One day he was a hero right in our backyard. (*Show the picture of Russell to the group. Ask the children what they remember about Russell.*)

One morning after it had rained all night, I let Russell out in the yard to play. He ran outside and headed for the back of the yard where he likes to sniff around the trees and grass. He was running across the cement patio like this (*Begin a rapid clapping rhythm.*) when all of a sudden he (*Make a sharp breaking sound.*) put on his brakes. Do you ever stop quickly like that? How does it sound? (*Allow several of the children to make their "braking sound."*) Then Russell did the strangest thing. He put his nose to the ground and began pushing something gently off the patio into my garden. I stepped out onto the patio to see what in the world that silly Russell was doing now. I looked closely and I saw that the patio was covered with these. (*Hold up several of the plastic worms.*) What are they? (*Allow the children time to answer.*) That's right. There were earthworms all over the patio and Russell was trying to push them back into the garden where they belonged. I began to help Russell and we carefully moved all of the worms off the patio. Once they were in the garden, Russell and I watched them quickly dig their way back into the soil. Once they disappeared I said, "Hustle, Russell, we need the facts. It is time to go to the library and find out more about these worms that you saved."

Discussing the Story

Now pass out the chewy worm-shaped candy and allow the children to eat them as they look at the materials you have collected. Share facts about earthworms from the "Fun Facts to Share" page. Ask for questions. If you do not know the answers for the questions, look them up with the children. Older students will be ready for longer and more detailed explanations and to look up information independently.

Integrating This Unit

- Introduce this unit in the spring in conjunction with one on gardening or the study of plants. Set up a patio or deck in your dramatic play area (see the Ants section). Move your sand/water table or a large plastic container into the area and fill it with some "Good Clean Fun Soil." (Stir together 1 bag of potting soil, 1 cup [240 mL] liquid starch, and $\frac{1}{2}$ cup [120 mL] dish detergent; add water if necessary.) Place some artificial flowers, plastic gardening tools, plastic pots, and plastic worms in the table/container. Encourage the children to plant a garden.

- In early spring, secure a small plot of land on the grounds of your facility and plant a small garden with the children. Have the children keep a record of the plants' growth through drawings and photos. Later add the students' comments about the garden to the pictures and make a class book to keep in your book area.

Interactive Display for Earthworms

Choose from the following:
- Picture of Russell
- Several pictures of earthworms
- Display a diagram of the worm's body parts
- Plastic or rubber models of worms obtained from a sporting goods store
- Place a few of the plastic worms in a container of potting soil and cover the worms with pieces of wood or rocks to illustrate how worms like to dig their burrows under these items where they are protected from light.
- Make a live display:
    1. Get a plastic or glass container (unused aquarium, plastic storage box).
    2. Place 2 in. (5 cm) of a gravel and stone mixture in the bottom for drainage.
    3. Layer 2 in. (5 cm) of soil between 2 in. (5 cm) sand until you have nearly reached the top of your container. Add a few rotting leaves and small pieces of decaying fruit skin to each layer of soil. Leave about 4 in. (10 cm) at the top.
    4. Moisten but do not soak the soil.
    5. Add the earthworms.
    6. Cover the top of your container with plastic wrap. Tape the wrap securely to the sides of the container and punch holes for air.
    7. Cover the sides of the container with dark cloth or paper and store in a dark place for three or four days.
    8. When you bring the display out for the children to observe, the layers will have been mixed up and the burrows that the worms have made will be visible.
- Fiction and nonfiction books about earthworms

Take Home Bag for Earthworms

Place one or more of the following items in each child's resealable plastic bag. Send the bag home following the introduction or at the end of the unit.

- Picture of Russell to encourage the children to retell the story
- Copy of "Fun Facts to Share" and a plastic or candy worm
- Photocopies of pictures taken of the live display
- Recipe for "Worms and Dirt" (page 19)
- Photocopy of any pictures taken during the "worm dig" or the dramatization

FUN FACTS to Share

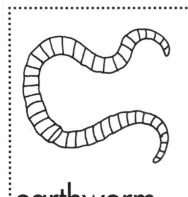

earthworm

About Its Body

- Earthworms have no ears. They feel vibrations with their whole bodies.
- Earthworms have no eyes, but they can tell light from dark.
- The earthworm has a mouth but no teeth.
- An earthworm's skin feels slimy. Oxygen passes through its damp skin right into the blood vessels.
- Its moist skin helps an earthworm to move through the burrows. If the skin dries out, the worm will die.
- The belly side of an earthworm feels rough. It has many bristles called setae.
- The giant Australian earthworm grows to 10 ft. (3m).

Food

- Earthworms feed on rotting plant parts.

Habitat

- Earthworms are found almost everywhere in the world. They are not in deserts where it is too dry. They are not in the polar regions either.
- An acre of good soil may be home to a million earthworms.

Habits

- In winter, the earthworm sleeps below the frost line.
- Earthworms spend all day underground. They come out at night to mate or find food.
- Worms sometimes eat soil. The soil goes through the worm's body. It exits as a pile of round balls called castings.
- Most earthworms live for less than a year, but some can live 10 years.
- Earthworms are eaten by animals like frogs, snakes, birds, moles, skunks, turtles, gophers, and fish.

Activities for Earthworms

- Have a "worm dig." Try to pick a cloudy day. Alert parents ahead of time about the dig and request that the children wear old clothes. Choose a shady area with a plot of ground where the children can dig easily (unplanted flower bed or garden). Dampen the soil a few hours before the dig. Supply the children with plastic garden shovels and collection bags. Use the worms found for your live display.

- Observe earthworms and record their length and color. Younger earthworms are shorter, thinner, and lighter in color. Which worms are probably the youngest? the oldest? Allow the children to examine the worms with magnifying glasses. Point out the head, tail, segments, damp skin, and the rougher skin of the belly. How can you tell the head from the tail? How does the skin feel on the top? On the belly? Do they know any other animal that has moist skin through which it breathes? (frog) What makes the belly of the earthworm feel slightly rough? Do these bristles help the worm?

- Invite the owner of a worm farm or a gardener to speak to your class about the value of earthworms.

- Have an indoor "worm hunt." Hide plastic worms around your room. Cut the "worms" into various lengths. Ask your students to each find a certain number of worms. Have the children count and measure their worms.

- Read aloud the book *Full Worm Moon* by Margo Lemieux (Tambourine Books, 1994) to the class. Dramatize the story using blankets and feathers as costumes for the family members and red and gold scarves or metallic yarn for the worms. Cut moon and sun shapes out of poster board. Cover the moon shape with tinfoil and paint the sun orange. Reread the story as the children act out their parts. Invite another group in to watch your play.

- Share this finger play about worms:
    Little worm crawled all around. (*Wiggle index finger.*)
    Digging tunnels underground. (*Wiggle index finger in downward motion.*)
    Then the rains came pouring down. (*Motion downward with both hands, fingers spread.*)
    Worm thought that he might drown. (*Wiggle index finger.*)
    But he floated up to the ground. (*Wiggle index finger in upward motion.*)
    Where he began to crawl around. (*Wiggle index finger.*)

- Make modeling dough or clay worms. Allow the worms to dry or fire and glaze the clay worms and use them as "pot sitters" in classroom plants or at home.

- Make a delicious "Worms and Dirt" snack. Have the children place some chocolate pudding in cups. Crush a cookie in a plastic bag and scatter the crumbs on top of the pudding. Add a chewy candy worm and enjoy!

- Investigate earthworms. As the following experiment is completed, take a photograph or have the children draw a picture for their class observation book. Record their comments on chart paper or have them record their observations in their notebooks. Complete the following investigations:

  A. How do earthworms hear? Darken your room. Place the live display where your group can clearly observe the earthworms' behavior. Play a musical instrument such as a flute near the worms. Is there any activity? Now place the worms on a piano where the vibrations can be felt by the worms. Play several notes sharply. Is there any activity? Allow the children to place their hands on the piano as you play. Discuss what they feel. These are the same vibrations that the worms feel as they pass through the soil. Vibrations warn worms of danger, such as a mole, nearby.

  B. Do earthworms prefer the light or the dark? Darken your room. Line the bottom of a shallow box with damp paper towels. Cover one half of the box with dark paper to keep out the light. Place one of the worms in the middle of the box. Shine a bright flashlight on the uncovered side of the box. Where does the worm go? Try this with other worms. Why do the worms choose the dark side of the box? How does this relate to where worms live?

  C. Do earthworms prefer dry or damp areas? Darken your room. Dampen a paper towel and spread it over the bottom of a shallow pan or tray. Cover the other half with a dry paper towel, overlapping the edges of the two towels. Place one of the worms near the overlapping edges. Where does the worm go? Try this with other worms. Why do worms choose the damp area? How does this relate to where worms live?

- Study a food chain. Cut pictures of a worm, frog, fish, and a person from magazines. Draw a thick black line across a rectangular piece of white paper, placing the pictures on the line in the order listed above. Explain how one animal provides food for another. Encourage the children to think of other food chains involving the earthworm, such as worm, small bird, and owl.

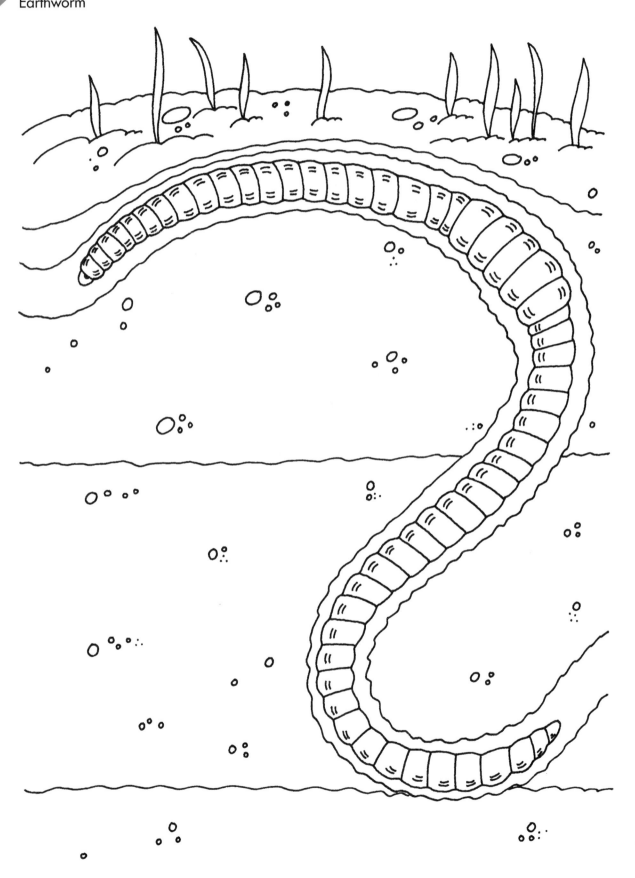

Food Chain

Earthworm

Frog

Fish

Human

Introducing Hermit Crabs

Children do not need to live near the beach to see hermit crabs. A common pet, they are easily obtained from local pet stores. Hermit crabs require little maintenance, making them an ideal animal for a science display in your classroom.

Suggested Visuals

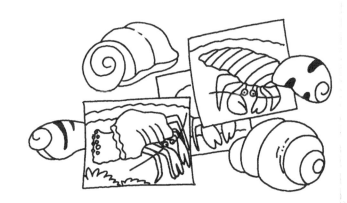

- Picture of Russell
- Three or four sizes of mollusk shells
- Full-color pictures of hermit crabs
- Live display of hermit crabs

 **Telling the Story**

Gather your students together for a story time. Bring one or more items from the Interactive Display but keep them covered. Hold up the picture of Russell and ask the children what they remember about Russell. Tell this story in your own words.

My dog Russell and I like to get up early while on vacation and go for walks on the beach. Russell loves to go on walks and is a great detective. He is not very brave, but he finds interesting things! (*Draw the children into the story by offering to show them a picture of your dog, Russell.*)

Every summer, Russell and I take a vacation. We always go to the beach. (*Ask the children if any of them has been to the beach. Have them share some of their experiences.*) One morning we went walking very early because some noisy birds woke Russell and me. Russell walks very fast. He walks this fast. (*Tap hands on thighs quickly.*) I don't walk that fast. I walk at this pace. (*Tap hands on thighs more slowly.*) Of course, I can run really fast. (*Tap hands accordingly.*)

Russell was walking his fast walk (*Make fast walking sound.*) and I was walking my slow walk. (*Make a slow walking sound.*) Russell was far ahead of me when I saw him put his nose to the ground and begin following something that was moving quickly across the beach. He barked the bark that means that I should catch up, so I started to run. (*Make a running sound.*) Russell was very close to the water when I reached him. He was barking at a shell. It looked like this. (*Show a shell.*) The shell began to move across the sand, making a kind of scratching sound. When Russell starts to bark like that I know that he is frightened. I bent down for a closer look, and I discovered that it was not just a shell. Inside, I could see a claw that belonged to some kind of animal. I guessed that this was the creature that had frightened Russell. I said, "Hustle, Russell, we need the facts. It is time to go to the library and find out about this animal that scared you."

Discussing the Story

Ask the children how they would describe the animal to the librarian when asking for information. Make a list of their descriptions. Introduce the pictures and/or live hermit crabs to the children, saying, "Here is the animal that was in that shell on the beach. Does anyone know what it is called?" Some of your students may know. If so, ask them to share what they know about hermit crabs.

As you show the group the hermit crabs, share some information from the "Fun Facts to Share" sheet. If you are showing your students the live crabs, add the mollusk shells to the aquarium. Sooner or later, the children will be treated to the sight of the crabs trying on and moving into new shells. Ask for questions. If you do not know the answers, look them up with the children. Older students will be able to look up their own answers and share them with the group later.

Integrating This Unit

• Combine this unit with one on travel. Have your class take a pretend trip to the beach.

• Study another kind of sea life that can be found living on or near the beach, such as sea turtles, who lay their eggs on the beach, or the small creatures that live in tide pools.

• Include a study of hermit crabs in a social studies unit on animal homes. Compare and contrast the various kinds of homes that animals create or use.

• Study several different kinds of crabs.

Interactive Display for Hermit Crabs

Choose from the following:
- Picture of Russell
- Several full-color pictures of hermit crabs
- Pictures of other kinds of crabs
- Crab shells from a pet store
- An assortment of shells for the children to sort and sequence according to size, type, and color
- "Ocean in a bottle" to demonstrate the action of waves. To make the model, fill the bottle half-full with water and add several drops of food coloring. Then fill the bottle to the top with vegetable oil. Screw the lid on tightly and cover it with duct tape to avoid leaks. Let the children tilt the bottle back and forth to create waves.
- "A look and feel" display: Fill a large plastic container with 2 to 3 in. (5 to 8 cm) of salted water, sand, seaweed, driftwood, and shells.
- Live display of hermit crabs
    1. Keep only one or two hermit crabs in an aquarium. The crabs should be of equal size with small claws. Be careful when handling them as they do pinch.
    2. Feed them fish food or hermit crab food available at a pet store.
    3. Read a book from a pet shop about the care of hermit crabs.
- Fiction and nonfiction books about hermit crabs and other crabs

Take Home Bag for Hermit Crabs

Place one or more of the following items in each child's resealable plastic bag. Send the bag home following the introduction or at the end of the unit.

- Picture of Russell to encourage the children to retell the story
- Copy of "Fun Facts to Share" and an interesting shell
- Photocopies of pictures taken of the live display
- Photocopies of any pictures taken during a dramatization

FUN FACTS to Share

hermit crab

About Its Body
- The hermit crab's skin is hard except for on its abdomen.
- A crab carries its shell around for protection.
- Hermit crabs differ from other crabs by having no armor of their own. They are in some danger when changing shells.
- Hermit crabs can move very quickly.
- The crab's eyes are located on the ends of flexible eye stalks.

Food
- Marine hermit crabs feed on sea lettuce, dead fish, and other small animals in tide pools.

Habitat
- There are different kinds of hermit crabs. Most are marine and live on the seashores. Some hermit crabs live on land.

Habits
- Land hermit crabs can climb. They are also called tree crabs.
- Hermit crabs are often called "Robber Crabs." They use the shells of other animals.
- Hermit crabs frequently seek new homes. They outgrow their old ones.
- Hermit crabs have been known to attach sea anemones to the outside of their shells, to detach them, and to take them with them when they move.
- The crab's antennae, claws, and two pairs of legs are outside of the shell when walking.
- If the crab is threatened, it will quickly withdraw the antennae, claws, and legs back into its shell.
- Its large claw is the last part to withdraw back into the shell. It acts like a door to close off the shell.

Activities for Hermit Crabs

- Introduce the live display at group time. Have a pet shop employee set up the live display and speak about how to care for hermit crabs. As he/she sets up the display, encourage the children to observe carefully and ask questions about what is in the tank, why the crabs need certain things, and what they will do with them.

  If it is not possible to have a live display, set out the tub/plastic container for the children to examine. For its first use, cover the tub containing the sand, shells, seaweed, driftwood, and saltwater with a box or towel so that the children will be able to slip their hands beneath. Place the tub in the center of the group and invite the children to place their hands in the water and describe what they feel. Encourage them to fist their hands in the sand and let it run through their fingers. Change the types of shells, driftwood, and seaweed in the water daily to create a slightly different tactile experience.

- Dramatize the story of a hermit crab's search for a new home. Read aloud the book *A House for Hermit Crab* by Eric Carle (Simon and Schuster, 1991) for the story line. Have the children make their own puppets. You will need: three snail shells of varying sizes, craft sticks, paper, pipe cleaners, and unused socks and/or gloves of various colors.

    Crab—Supply a dark glove/sock for the crab's body. Affix two large eyes and some red
        pipe cleaners for legs.
    Sea anemones—Use green socks and attach strips of brightly colored paper to the ends.
        Add eyes for personality.
    Starfish—Attach a star-shaped cutout to the end of a craft stick.
    Coral—Use brown gloves with an eye on each finger.
    Sea urchins—Attach several pipe cleaners to the ends of craft sticks.
    Lantern fish—Use a black glove holding a black flashlight. Place one large eye on the
        light.
    Stones—Attach eyes to a few stones and have the puppeteers hold the stones while
        wearing black, gray, or white gloves or socks on their hands.

- Read aloud the book *Is This a House for Hermit Crab?* by Megan McDonald (Orchard Books, 1993). Collect the items shown in the book: a shell, rock, tin can, driftwood, sand pail, hole in the sand (glue some sand on a piece of cardboard leaving a hole in the center), a tangle of rope, and new shell. As you hold up each item, ask the children if it would make a good home for a hermit crab.

- Learn about seaweed. Seaweed can be found all along the seashore. (The fish department in your local grocery store or an Oriental restaurant or grocery may be able to supply you with some.) They have special roots called "holdfasts" that cling to rocks. Collect some seaweed and put it in a see-through container. Use a stone to hold it on the bottom of the container. Add water. Examine the shape of the seaweed when it is held up by the water. Note how it goes limp out of the water.

- Have children sort a large collection of shells into groups according to size, color, and/or kind.

- Play "Shadow Shell Match." Tape several interesting shells on a sheet of white paper with the name of the shell written underneath on the paper. Place shells and paper in the photocopy machine. Close the lid and copy. Cover the paper with plastic film or laminate it for continued use. Place the paper and the shells on the science table for continued matching fun.

- Make individual "oceans in a bottle." These are smaller versions of the one recommended for the Interactive Display. Use baby food jars or plastic soda bottles. Have the children follow the same recipe. Be sure to tape or glue the top.

- Here is a finger play for hermit crabs:
  (*Discuss the meaning of the expression "pell-mell" before starting.*)
  Mr. Hermit Crab is snug in his shell. (*Close fist snugly over opposite index finger.*)
  There he grows until . . . (*Open fist slowly, extending finger.*)
  He has to move pell-mell! (*Index and middle fingers scurry away quickly.*)

  Mr. Hermit Crab finds a new shell (*Close fist snugly over opposite index finger.*)
  There he grows until . . . (*Open fist slowly, extending finger.*)
  He has to move pell-mell! (*Index and middle fingers scurry away quickly.*)

- Make an underwater viewer by cutting off the bottom two-thirds of a clear plastic bottle. Cover the sharp edge with tape. Put plastic wrap tightly over the large open end and secure it with a rubber band. Put the covered end in the water and look down into the water and view through the opening at the top (see illustration below).

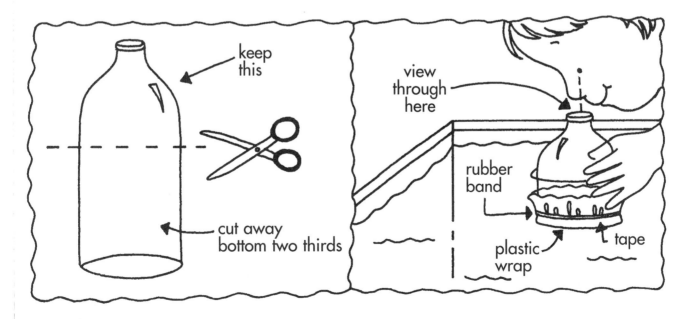

keep this

cut away bottom two thirds

view through here

rubber band

plastic wrap

tape

Is this a good home for a hermit crab?

	Yes	No
shell		
tin can		
rock		
sand bucket		
drift wood		
hole in the sand		

Introducing Monarch Butterflies

Monarch butterflies exist almost everywhere in the United States. Young children are attracted to their bright colors. It is fascinating to watch how the monarch caterpillar changes into a butterfly.

Suggested Visuals

- Picture of Russell
- Full-color pictures of monarch butterflies
- Model of a monarch butterfly
- Flower from a lilac bush, purple coneflower plant, goldenrod, or thistle

 **Telling the Story**

Gather your students together for a story time. Bring one or more items from the Interactive Display but keep them covered. Hold up the picture of Russell and ask the children what they remember about Russell. Tell this story in your own words.

Usually, Russell and I go for a walk every day, but sometimes we feel like taking a run. Do you ever feel like running? How do your feet sound when you run? (*Tap your hands on your thighs and encourage the children to join you in creating a running sound rhythm—a slow running pace, a fast running pace, and the fastest run of all.*)

Yesterday morning Russell and I went for a long run. First we ran around our block and then around once more. I started running fast like this. (*Make fast running sound.*) Russell runs much faster than I do and he was running like this. (*Make fastest running sound.*) After a while, I began to get tired and had to slow down. (*Make slow running sound.*) Finally I was so tired that I slowed to a walk. (*Make a slow walking rhythm.*) Russell must have been feeling really good because he ran the whole way like this. (*Make fastest running sound.*)

I know that Russell was tired when we returned home because he took a nap while I planted some flowers in my garden. Then Russell began to snore. What a funny sound! It sounded like this. (*Make a snoring sound.*) When I looked at the dog, I saw a beautiful creature with orange, yellow, and black wings sitting on Russell's head. Russell must have felt the tiny creature because he began to shake his head. As he shook his head, the tiny animal flew away and landed on some weeds near where I was planting flowers.

Russell jumped to his feet and began chasing the colorful creature. (*Make the fastest running sound.*) He ran right through my newly planted garden, uprooting the plants, and getting his feet all dirty. Meanwhile that tiny animal had fluttered it wings as it headed over to the top of our (lilac bushes, goldenrod, or thistle) and stayed there. This is what the plant looked like. (*Hold up an example of a lilac, goldenrod, or thistle flower, depending on what is in season.*) I shouted,

"You'll never catch that creature, Russell. It can fly and you can't." Russell hung his head and slowly walked back to me. (*Make walking sounds.*) I said, "Hustle, Russell, we need the facts. After I get you cleaned up, we are going to the library to find out about an animal that lands on sleeping dogs and likes flowers."

Discussing the Story

Ask the students to describe the animal that Russell chased. Make a list of their descriptions. Now show the pictures and the model of the monarch butterfly. Explain that this is the animal that Russell was chasing. What is it called? The children will recognize a butterfly but will probably need help with the name "monarch butterfly." Point out the special colors on the monarch's wings. As the children look at the materials you have collected, share some of the information from the "Fun Facts to Share" sheet with them. Ask for questions. If you do not know the answers, look them up together. Older children will be ready for longer and more detailed explanations.

Integrating This Unit

- Try combining the study of the monarch butterfly with the study of a migratory bird such as the robin or the Canadian goose.

- Combine this unit with one on plants. Try transplanting milkweed plants to attract monarch butterflies.

- Compare and contrast the life cycle of a butterfly with that of another animal, such as a frog, that changes form with the different stages of its development.

Interactive Display for Monarch Butterflies

Choose from the following:
- Pictures of monarch caterpillar, butterfly, egg, and chrysalis
- Pictures showing the butterfly's life cycle
- Model of the monarch butterfly. These can be found in nature and/or teacher catalogs.
- Goldenrod, lilacs, or thistle flower, and milkweed leaves on stems
- Candy sticks with white, yellow, and black rings
- Map to show the migratory route that the monarch butterfly would follow from your state to Mexico/California
- Live display:
    1. Poke several holes in a box.
    2. Fill a large jar with water. Make several holes in the lid.
    3. Collect some milkweed leaves (preferably leaves that have eggs attached to them) with stems. Put the stems through the holes in your jar so that they can reach the water.
    4. Put the jar with the leaves in a large box.
    5. Place some monarch caterpillars on the milkweed leaves.
    6. Cover the open end of the box with clear plastic and tape over the edges.
    7. Watch the caterpillars each day. Make sure they have enough milkweed leaves and keep the box out of direct sunlight. In time, each caterpillar will change into a chrysalis. When butterflies emerge, do not touch them. If possible, remove the box or just the plastic cover and let the butterflies fly away.
- Fiction and nonfiction books about butterflies

Take Home Bag for Monarch Butterflies

Place one or more of the following items in each child's resealable plastic bag. Send the bag home following the introduction or at the end of the unit.

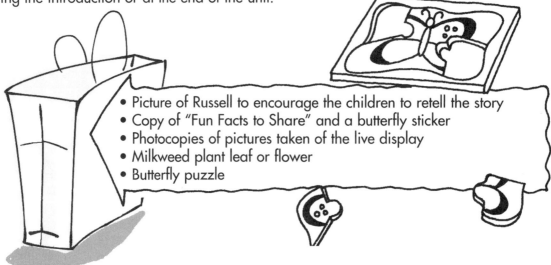

- Picture of Russell to encourage the children to retell the story
- Copy of "Fun Facts to Share" and a butterfly sticker
- Photocopies of pictures taken of the live display
- Milkweed plant leaf or flower
- Butterfly puzzle

FUN FACTS to Share

monarch butterfly

About Its Body

- The butterfly's body has three main parts: the head, the thorax, and the abdomen.
- On its head are large eyes, antennae, and a long tube for drinking.
- Butterflies look like they have two wings. They have four.
- Its wings are bright orange and black with white dots set in a black border.
- Monarch caterpillars look like a candy stick with white, yellow, and black rings.

Foods

- Monarch butterflies like to feed on flowers, especially lilacs, thistle, goldenrod, purple coneflowers, and marigolds.
- Monarch caterpillars feed only on the leaves of milkweed plants.

Habitat

- Monarch butterflies live in areas where milkweed plants can be found.

Habits

- Monarchs lay their eggs on milkweed leaves. After three or four days, the caterpillar hatches. First it eats its eggshell, then it begins to eat the milkweed leaves.
- When the caterpillar grows too big for its skin, the old skin splits open. Underneath is another bigger skin. This happens four or five times. After the skin splits for the last time, the caterpillar changes into a chrysalis.
- Monarch butterflies migrate to a warmer place for the winter. Those living east of the Rocky Mountains fly to Mexico year after year. Those living west of the mountains travel to places in California.

Activities for Monarch Butterflies

- Make a moving caterpillar. Cut several 1 in. x 12 in. (3 cm x 30 cm) strips of white paper and divide them into 1 in. (3 cm) squares. Instruct the children to color the squares to resemble a monarch caterpillar, following a yellow, white, and black pattern. Fold the strips accordion style and have the children shorten and lengthen their caterpillars as they move them across a table.

- Read the book *The Very Hungry Caterpillar* by Eric Carle (Putnam Publishers, 1971). Cut the shapes of the food that the caterpillar ate from large pieces of colored construction paper. Make a hole in the center of each shape. (Laminate for continued use.) One student should hold up each shape. Have one child (the caterpillar) hold a piece of material or scarf (yellow, white, and black if possible). As the story is read aloud once more, have the child pull the scarf through each piece of food as the story dictates. Repeat until each child has played a part.

- Gather milkweed leaves and several other kinds of leaves that are common to your area. Have the children compare the leaves. Provide photocopies of the leaves and have the children match each leaf to its "shadow." Leave the materials in the interactive display area. (Laminate leaves or dip them in melted paraffin wax, so they will keep longer.)

- Compare foods with bitter and sweet tastes. Which do students prefer? Which would the caterpillar's enemies prefer?

- Create models for life cycle kits. To make the models, have the child form a caterpillar out of modeling dough or other molding material. Wrap a peanut shell with green yarn to represent the chrysalis. For the model of a monarch butterfly, slip orange and black tissue paper into a clothespin. Add eyes with a marker and affix a pipe cleaner for antennae. If appropriate, the child can proudly carry home the kit in the Take Home Bag.

- Dramatize the life cycle of a butterfly. If possible, provide each child with two brightly colored scarves and encourage them to use the scarves in each part of the movement activity. First, have the children curl up tightly to represent an egg. Then have the children stretch out on the floor and pretend to be a caterpillar. How do caterpillars move? The caterpillars should munch as they move around the floor. Then have the children stand and spin a chrysalis. After they have been very still for a couple of seconds, have them pretend to break out of the chrysalis and spread their butterfly wings. Take pictures and photocopy them for the Take Home Bag.

- Make colorful monarch butterflies to hang in your room. Fold a piece of black construction paper in fourths. Draw a line that shows where to cut for a butterfly shape. Cut several interesting shapes into the folded shape. Open the shape and place it on wax paper. Paint over the holes with colored school glue. Allow the shape to dry, attach a string, and hang the colorful butterflies in your window.

- Make butterfly gloom chasers for your windows. Cut out a butterfly shape for each child out of wax paper. Have the children fill in the entire shape with colored glue. When the glue dries (this may take several days), peel away the wax paper and stick the butterflies on a classroom window or save the project for the Take Home Bag. These also make good gifts for parents.

- Drink like a butterfly. Attached to the butterfly's head is a long tube for drinking called a proboscis. Have the students connect three or four drinking straws together to make one long straw. At snack time, fill their glasses with fruit juice and have the children suck the juice through the long straw.

- Draw the missing half. Note how the wings of a butterfly appear to be reflections of each other. Demonstrate this by holding a mirror vertically along the center of the picture of the butterfly (see page 36). Cover one half the butterfly before making a copy of the pattern for each child. If possible provide each child with a mirror and a copy of the illustration and encourage her to draw (from the reflection) the other half of the butterfly.

- Pretend to be butterflies. If possible, supply the children with one or two colorful scarves or pieces of material. Pick one child to be the butterfly. The other children curl up into balls on the floor with their eyes closed. They are caterpillars waiting to emerge from their chrysalises. When everyone is ready, the butterfly taps one or two of the caterpillars lightly on the shoulder and they transform into butterflies, fluttering around the room. Repeat until all the butterflies emerge.

wrap in toilet tissue

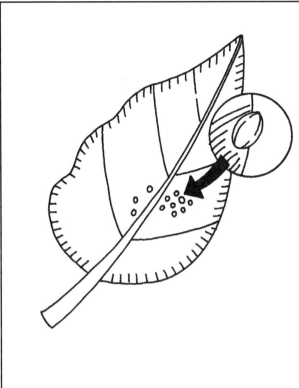

egg

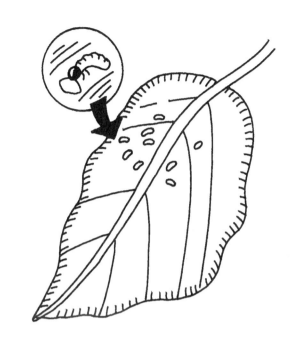

larva

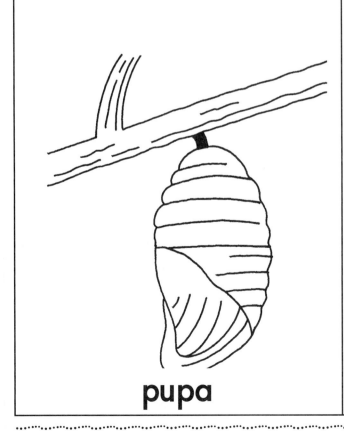

pupa

butterfly

Introducing Bats

Even young children have heard some of the myths about the mysterious night creature, the bat. A study of bats will reveal the true facts about these helpful animals. Like spiders, bats help to keep the insect population under control.

Suggested Visuals

- Picture of Russell
- Pictures of various kinds of bats
- Rubber or plastic model of a bat
- Empty jar
- Pictures of a lightning bug
- Crayons and drawing paper

 **Telling the Story**

Gather your students together for a story time. Bring one or more items from the Interactive Display but keep them covered. Hold up the picture of Russell and ask the children what they remember about Russell. Tell this story in your own words.

Russell and I were too busy to take a walk yesterday until the sun was going down. By then, we were tired, so we decided to just go out in the yard after dark and have fun catching some lightning bugs. Have you ever caught any lightning bugs? (*Take some time to listen to the children's answers/comments. Very young children may need to see a picture of a lightning bug.*)

Russell likes to chase things, and he is very helpful at catching lightning bugs. He watches for the bugs to light up and then chases after them. I run after him and catch the bugs in a jar like this. (*Hold up a jar.*) Sometimes we catch several lightning bugs at one time. We watch how the bugs inside the jar glow in the dark, and then we let them go.

Last night while we were out in the yard, I noticed that there were an awful lot of mosquitoes flying around us. I kept swatting at them and Russell was shaking his head—like this (*Shake your head and encourage the children to join in.*) Then he began to run in a big circle around the yard—trying to escape the pesky mosquitoes. (*Tap your hands against your thighs with a quick running rhythm and encourage the children to join in.*) Have you ever been outside where a lot of mosquitoes were trying to bite you? Does it hurt? How does it feel after they bite? What do you do for the bites? (*Take some time for the children to share their experience with mosquitoes.*) I said to Russell, "Let's go in! I am getting eaten alive! These mosquitoes are even trying to bite you." Just then I saw a big, fat mosquito hovering near Russell's nose. Before it could land and bite Russell, something dark and quick swept down out of the sky and gobbled it up!

Russell only saw a swish of darkness close to his nose. It scared him, and he ran to the back door as fast as he could. (*Begin a very quick running rhythm and encourage the children to join in.*) As I opened the door to let him come into the house, I said, "Hustle, Russell, we need the facts. First thing tomorrow we are going to the library to find out about a creature that sweeps down out of the sky at night to eat mosquitoes!"

Discussing the Story

Ask if any of the children know the name of this creature that swept down out of the sky. Ask them to describe the creature and then draw a picture of what they think the mosquito-eating animal looked like. Share the pictures with the group.

Now show the children the pictures/models that you have collected. "Here is the animal that scared Russell. What is it called?" If the children do not know what the animal is, tell them it is a bat and explain how bats are very helpful creatures.

Point out the special features of bats. As the children examine the materials you have collected, share facts from the "Fun Facts to Share" page. Ask for questions. If you do not know the answers, look them up together. Older students will be ready for longer and more detailed explanations.

Integrating This Unit

- Combine this unit with one on spiders, who also help with insect control in their own unique way.

- Present this unit in October and offer the children the real facts about a very interesting animal that has traditionally been connected with Halloween.

Interactive Display for Bats

Choose from the following:
- Several pictures of bats
- Rubber or plastic models of bats
- A diorama from a nature center or lending museum
- A bat house from a nature center or lending museum
- A penny and a 2-pound (.9 kg) weight to represent the weight of the smallest and the largest bat. Supply a balance scale and some other classroom objects so that the children can make comparisons.
- Fill a jar or bowl with 600 raisins or another small food to represent the number of mosquitoes that one bat can eat in an hour.
- Fiction and nonfiction books about bats

Take Home Bag for Bats

Place one or more of the following items in each child's resealable plastic bag. Send the bag home following the introduction or at the end of the unit.

- Photocopy of Russell to encourage the children to retell the story
- Copy of "Fun Facts to Share" and a bat sticker
- Photocopy of one of the bat pictures from the display
- Photocopy of any pictures that you took on your trip to the zoo or pictures from the dramatization of the book *Stellaluna* by Jannell Cannon (Harcourt Brace, 1993)

FUN FACTS to Share

bat

About Its Body
- Bats are the only mammals that can fly.
- Bats have fur to keep them warm in cold weather. Their wings are like skin stretched over their arms.
- Bats have little thumbs that are claw-like and help them move over the rough surfaces of tree bark or cave walls.
- Bats hang upside down. This is called roosting.
- The smallest bat, the bumblebee bat, is as big as a bee and weighs less than a penny.
- The largest bat, the Samoan flying fox, has a wingspan of approximately 6.5 feet (2 meters) and weighs about 2 pounds (0.9 kilograms).

Food
- Most bats are insect eaters and feed on beetles, flies, moths, and mosquitoes. Others feed on nectar from flowers.

Habitat
- Most bats live in caves because they are dark and quiet. They also roost in tall trees, barns, attics, bushes, and fence posts.
- There are nearly one thousand different species (kinds) of bats in the world. They are found in more climates and habitats than almost any other animal.

Habits
- Bats catch insects by making a noise when flying: click, click, click. When an insect flies by, the click bounces off it like an echo, telling the bat where the insect is.
- A bat needs to eat a lot because it uses so much energy when it flies. A bat can catch and eat 600 mosquitoes in an hour.
- Bats stay awake at night (nocturnal). During the day, they sleep hanging upside down.

Activities for Bats

- Discuss bats and compare them with other animals. At group time, have the children take a good look at the bat in the diorama and make a list of the unique features that a bat has. What features do bats have in common with other animals? What is different about them? What is the bat's habitat? After the children have taken a good look at bats, ask them what it is about bats that makes them frightening to some people. Discuss myths about bats.

- How much does the largest bat weigh? Pass around pictures of a variety of different kinds of bats. Next pass around a penny and explain that it is the weight of the smallest bat. Then pass around a 2 lb. (0.9 kg) weight, informing the children that it is the weight of the largest bat. Put a balance scale in the middle of your group. Place both items on the scale. Which one is heavier? How can they tell? Now remove the penny and have the children find classroom objects that they think might weigh as much as the 2 lb. (.9 kg) weight. Have each child place their object on the scale to see if it weighs more, less, or the same. Repeat this activity, replacing the weight with the penny.

- Present the jar of raisins to the class, noting that it is filled with the same number as the number of mosquitoes that some bats can eat in an hour. Have each child estimate the number. Record everyone's estimate. If it is appropriate, have the children identify the highest and lowest estimates or put all of the estimates in order from highest to lowest. Either count out or tell the children the actual number. Host a special "mosquito-eating" party. Open the jar of raisins and allow each child to have several. Have them count to see how many mosquitoes each will eat.

- Observe bats and other night creatures in your local zoo.

- Move like a bat. Provide a variety of both sheer and heavy black cloths that are about 18 in. (46 cm) long. Have the children hold the cloths and pretend to be bats, swooping to find their dinner.

- Make a cave by draping a dark sheet or blanket over one of your tables. See how many "bats" can fit in your cave.

- Make a True-False chart. Use the bat myths below along with some true statements from "Fun Facts to Share." Write each on a large piece of chart paper, leaving a space next to each statement. Have the children make happy faces next to the true statements and sad faces next to the false (or write true/false). There are many myths about bats that make some people think they are bad. Some include:
    a. Bats are flying mice or rats. Not true. Bats are their own species, unrelated to rodents.
    b. Bats have evil powers because witches use their wings to make witches' brew. Not true. Bats are no different than other animals.

    c. Bats are blind. Not true. Bats see very well even in the darkest places. Some bats see with their eyes. Other bats "see" where they are going by echolocation.

    d. Bats like to get tangled in people's hair. Not true. Bats have no interest in hair.

    e. Bats are dirty animals. Not true. Bats are clean animals that spend a lot of time grooming.

    f. All bats carry rabies. Not true. Like any wild animal, bats can get rabies, but most bats do not have rabies.

    g. Vampire bats like to suck the blood of humans. Not true. Vampire bats feed on sleeping animals, such as cows or horses.

- Create some echoes. Try different locations in your building, such as stairwells, playground, classroom, and hallways, to create echoes . Have the children try this at home and report back to the class on their results.

- Read the book *Stellaluna* by Janell Cannon (Harcourt Brace, 1993) to your group. Have the children take turns playing the parts of Narrator, Mother Bat, Stellaluna, Owl, Flap, Fritter, Pip, Mama bird, and other bats. For costumes, have the children playing bats wear black scarves that have been pinned to their sides and under their arms. Glue real or child-made feathers to arm-length strips of paper. Tape these strips to the arms of the birds. For Owl, make a paper headband and glue a beak shape and some dark feather shapes to it.

- Sort animals by skin covering. Place a selection of plastic or stuffed animals in your display area. Have the children sort the animals into two categories, such as mammals and other creatures or animals with fur and animals without fur.

- Make a dimensional bat. Use the pattern on page 45 to make your bat. Cut the body and wings out of black construction paper. Put the wings through the slit in the body. Attach an elastic string to the underside to have your bat hang upside-down.

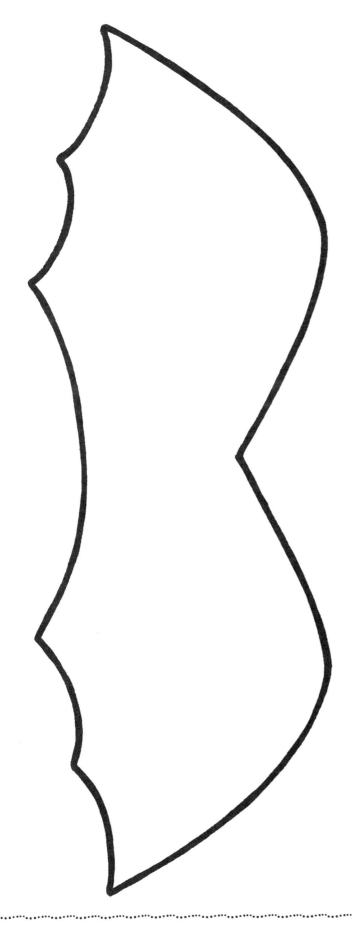

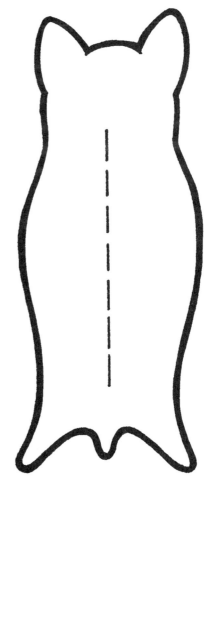

Introducing Bears

Some young children have seen bears at the zoo or while visiting a national park. However, most children's experiences with these animals is through toys, stories, and cartoons that portray bears as cuddly and friendly. Although bears may look adorable and sweet, they loose their tempers quickly and can become dangerous. The bear's worst enemy is man. Man's desire for more land and resources is giving bears less space in which to live and find food. Young children will enjoy learning about bears, their habits, and some of the problems that they have.

Suggested Visuals

- Picture of Russell
- Pictures of campsites
- Pictures of bear habitat
- Pictures of the seven kinds of bears (Alaskan brown [Kodiak and grizzly bears], American black, Asiatic black, polar, sloth, spectacled, and Malayan)
- Stuffed toy bears or carvings of bears
- Large chart paper and marker

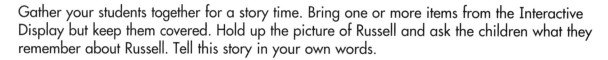

 **Telling the Story**

Gather your students together for a story time. Bring one or more items from the Interactive Display but keep them covered. Hold up the picture of Russell and ask the children what they remember about Russell. Tell this story in your own words.

Early last spring Russell and I went on a camping trip with some friends. Our campsite was in a huge park in the foothills of a mountain. There were many wonderful things to see. (*If possible, show the children some pictures of campgrounds.*) We camped in this special place for one week. Russell loves to camp because he gets to sleep in a tent and we go on long walks every day. Russell is a great detective—especially on camping trips. Even though Russell is not very brave, he has some exciting adventures.

On the last morning of our camping trip, Russell and I went for a long walk. We hiked up a very steep hill. It was a difficult climb. Then we walked through dark woods. The cool air felt refreshing. Finally we stopped at a cave entrance. Russell was very excited about seeing a cave. He was walking his very fastest walk. Do you remember how Russell walks? (*Wait to see what they remember.*) His fast walk is very fast, like this. (*Tap hands on thighs with fast rhythm.*) I usually walk like this. (*Tap hands on thighs in a slower rhythm.*) However, I had to run to keep up with Russell that day. (*Tap hand on thighs in a running rhythm.*)

46

Russell stopped near the entrance of the cave to wait for me. I do not think that he wanted to go in that dark cave by himself. When I reached the entrance, I turned on my flashlight and pointed the beam of light deep into the cave. Russell had just peeked into the cave when we heard a loud growling sound like this. (*Make a very loud growling sound.*) Russell was too scared to make a sound. He just tucked his tail between his legs and ran back toward our campsite. I was right behind him. We were both running faster than we had ever run before (*Tap hands against your thighs very quickly.*) and breathing hard like this (*Mimic labored breathing.*) While we were running back to our campsite, we came upon one of the park's rangers. Boy, were we ever glad to see him! When I told him about the growling sound that Russell and I had heard coming from the cave, he said, "You better hustle with Russell to the library to learn about animals that live in caves and how to keep yourself safe in the woods." Do you know what? That is exactly what we did.

Discussing the Story

Ask the children if they can guess what animal was in the cave. If the children suggest that the animal is a bear, say, "I thought that it was a bear, too." Ask, "What made you think it was a bear?" Then record the reasons. Introduce the pictures, toy bears, and/or carvings of bears. Ask the group what they know about bears and write down their answers on a large piece of chart paper. Share some of the facts about bears from the "Fun Facts to Share" page. Ask for questions. If you do not know the answers, look them up together. Older students will be able to look up their own answers and share them with the group later.

Integrating This Unit

- This unit would work well with the study of camping and nature/survival skills. Set up a campsite in your room using a tent, a "campfire" with stones and logs, some outdoor cooking utensils, and any other camping accoutrements that are available to you. Have the children pretend to be camping in a huge forest where bears might live. Make some plans together about how to stay safe while camping and enjoying the outdoors.

- Include the study of other animals that live in the same areas that bears do, such as deer and timber wolves. Compare and contrast the species. How are they alike? How are they different? What does each do in the winter?

- Combine this unit with a study of Native Americans. What important part did the bear play in their everyday life, legends, and art?

Interactive Display for Bears

Choose from the following:

- Picture of Russell
- Pictures of the various kinds of bears from books and/or the Internet
- Statues or carvings of bears
- Enlarged bear tracks drawn on poster board
- Plastic models of animal paws
- Nuts and dried berries that bears would to eat
- Live insects that bears would eat
- Abandoned bee's nest
- Pictures of fish or a stuffed fish
- Container of honey and some ice cream sticks for tasting
- Make a bear cave near your display using a dark blanket over a table or a large appliance box. Provide the children with a flashlight to check on any "hibernating bears."
- Large piece of faux bear's fur
- World map marked to indicate where various kinds of bears live
- Picture of the Great Bear and Little Bear Constellations
- Fiction and nonfiction books about bears

Take Home Bag for Bears

Place one or more of the following items in each child's resealable plastic bag. Send the bag home following the introduction or at the end of the unit.

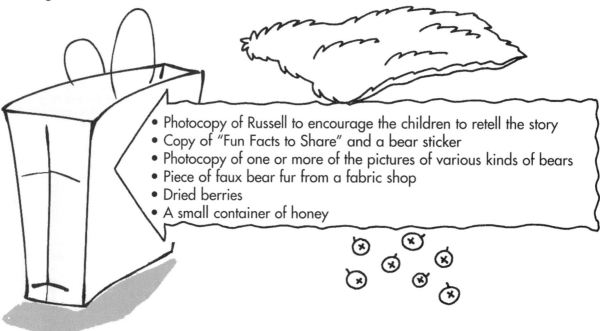

- Photocopy of Russell to encourage the children to retell the story
- Copy of "Fun Facts to Share" and a bear sticker
- Photocopy of one or more of the pictures of various kinds of bears
- Piece of faux bear fur from a fabric shop
- Dried berries
- A small container of honey

FUN FACTS to Share

bear

About Its body
- There are seven kinds of bears: American black bears, brown bears, polar bears, sun bears, spectacled bears, sloth bears, and Asiatic black bears.
- All bears have five toes and five claws on each foot.
- Bears have a keen sense of smell and good hearing.
- All bears can swim, although polar bears are the strongest swimmers. A bear's front feet are webbed like a duck's feet.
- Cubs are born with their eyes closed and they cannot walk. They weigh about 1 pound (0.5 kilograms) but grow very quickly on the rich milk of their mother.

Food
- All bears have powerful jaws and teeth for eating different kinds of food. They eat stems and roots, raw meat, fish, and nuts. Bears also eat insects, fruit, honey, and leaves.

Habitat
- Bears live on the continents of Asia, North and South America, and Europe. Most bears live in forests, except for polar bears that roam the Arctic ice pack and tundra.

Habits
- Bears may look sweet and cuddly but they can loose their temper quickly and become dangerous.
- Bears make caring mothers. Mother bears keep their babies (cubs) with them until the bears are about two years old.
- Like humans, bears put their feet down flat on the ground when they walk. This makes it easy for them to stand up and walk on their hind legs. Most other large animals walk on their toes.
- Sometime during the fall season, American black bears and brown bears find caves or dig holes in the ground or snow to make dens. Later, they crawl into their dens to sleep, off and on, all winter. This kind of sleep is called hibernation.

Activities for Bears

- Spend time in the classroom cave. Gather the children together for a group time in the cave. Ask some questions that will heighten their curiosity and encourage them to draw conclusions. For example: What do caves have to do with bears? What do bears do in the winter? How do bears get ready for winter? What foods do bears eat? Do bears sometimes wake up on warmer days in the winter or when they are disturbed? How do you think they feel?

- Take a field trip to your city zoo to observe bears. To make the tour more informative, ask for a zoo docent who is knowledgeable about bears to join your group.

- Read the book *Blueberries for Sal* by Robert McClosky (Penguin Putnam, 1976). Explain that in 1948 canning was an important way to preserve fresh fruits and vegetables to eat in the winter. Discuss the parallel between the bears fattening up for their winter sleep and people preparing food for winter. Are there any times when people stock up on food supplies today? What are they? What other animal(s) gathers food for winter?

- Make blueberry jam with the children. You will need:
    4 cups (948 mL) washed fresh blueberries (or any other fresh berry)
    3 cups (711 mL) sugar
    Enough water to keep the berries from burning
    1 large heavy pan (electric frying pan will work)
Crush the fruit and add just enough water to keep the fruit from burning. Cook until soft. Dissolve the sugar in the fruit mixture. Bring the mixture to a full boil until it is clear and thick, about 8–10 minutes. Remove the jam from the heat and allow it to cool. Enjoy it on bread or toast.

- Read the book *We're Going on a Bear Hunt* by Michael Rosen (Simon and Schuster, 1992) to your group. Divide the class into groups of four or five to dramatize the story. Create your own sound effects or use the following ideas: grass—brush a hand broom across the top of a drum; river—splash hand in a bucket of water; mud—suck a small amount of water out of a dish with a meat baster; forest—clap two sticks together; and snowstorm—shake a piece of tin foil.

- Make paw prints. Place a flat foam tray underneath the drawing of a bear paw print from the science center. Trace around the outside of the entire print with a pencil with no lead or a ballpoint pen that has run out of ink. Press hard enough to leave a visible line in the tray. Cut out the shape from the foam. Make the toes visible by carving deep lines where the toes should be. Dab into paint and press onto paper to make prints.

- Make sand castings from the rubber/plastic models of bear paws.

- Make a "Do Bears . . . ?" chart. Using a large piece of lined chart paper, write several questions about bears, one per line.
  For example:

  Do bears eat honey?
  Do bears eat insects?
  Do bears live in houses?
  Do bears swim?
  Do bears walk on tiptoe?
  Do bears hibernate?
  Do bears bark?

  Have the children draw a frown face for "no" and a smile face for "yes" on the line following each question.

- Perform the finger play "The Little Bears." (*Hold all five fingers up.*)
  This little bear just wants to sleep. (*Lower thumb.*)
  But this little bear wants to eat! (*Lower pointer finger.*)
  This little bear is awfully tall. (*Lower middle finger.*)
  And this little bear is kind of small. (*Lower ring finger.*)
  This little bear is a baby yet. (*Lower little finger.*)
  But don't ever think that he's a pet! (*Shake head no.*)

- Read the book *The Three Bears* by Paul Galdone (Houghton Mifflin, 1985). Have the group act out the story using three different-sized chairs, three-different sized bowls, and three-different sized boxes covered with blankets. Afterward, draw or photocopy pictures of several household items. Using the enlarging function on the copy machine, photocopy each in three or more sizes for your students to sequence.

- Talk about the Great and Little Bear constellations. Ask the children if any of them have looked at the stars at night. Show the class some pictures of several constellations and name them. Explain how the early Greeks named the stars and their constellations. Ask if any of them have seen these pictures in the sky. Photocopy the pattern of the constellations on page 53. Have the children place a star sticker on each dot. Connect the dots.

- Show a picture of President Theodore Roosevelt. Explain that his nickname was Teddy. Tell them that this is the man for whom the teddy bear was named. This is how it happened: It was in 1902, and Theodore Roosevelt was our President. Once, when he was out hunting, he refused to shoot a black bear. President Roosevelt was so popular that lots of toy bears were created to celebrate this event. They were called teddy bears after the President. Have a teddy bear picnic in your classroom. Invite each child to bring in a teddy bear. Spread some blankets on the floor for students and teddy bears. Serve foods that bears like to eat, such as bread and honey sandwiches, fresh berries, and nuts.

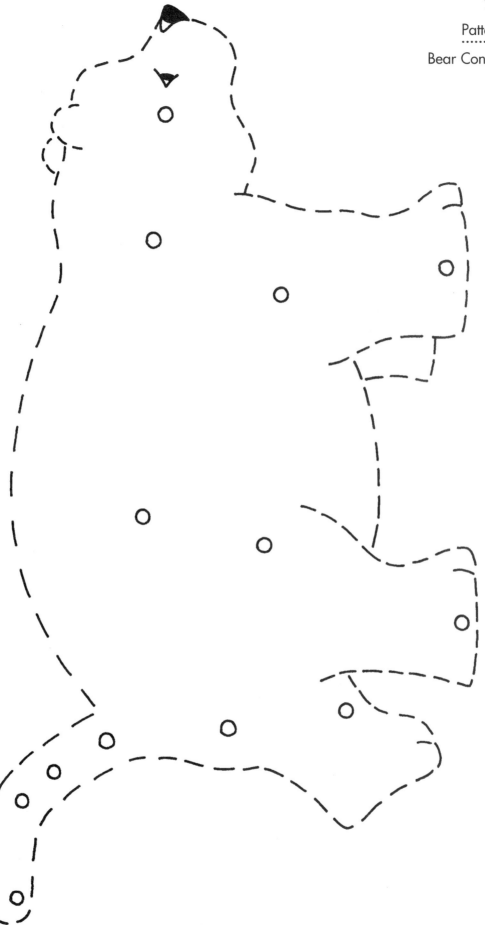

53

Introducing Skunks

Although most children have only seen skunks from a safe distance, many are familiar with the odor associated with them. Children relate to this concrete means of defense and will be drawn to learn more about these easily identifiable and appealing animals.

Suggested Visuals

- Picture of Russell
- Several full-color pictures of skunks
- Cotton ball dipped in musk oil

 **Telling the Story**

Gather your students together for a story time. Bring several items suggested from the Interactive Display, but keep them covered until after the story. Tell the following story in your own words.

I have to tell you what happened to Russell the other day. You know how Russell likes to poke and sniff (*Wiggle nose and sniff.*) like a detective, right? Well, it was late one evening when Russell and I went outside to take out the garbage. I started to walk back inside the house, but Russell was busy sniffing the ground. I let him stay outside a little longer. Sometimes, when I'm not with Russell he starts to dig with his paws like this (*Show digging action.*), and he even has been able to get under the fence and into the woods that way.

I think that's what must have happened that night because the next thing I knew, I heard a howl like this (*Can you howl?*) and Russell came running with a great burst of speed. (*Demonstrate fast running noise on knees.*) Before he even got to the door, I knew what happened. I could smell something very strong. In fact, I think the whole neighborhood could smell it—and it was not perfume.

"Hustle, Russell," I said. "We have to clean you off! Whew! After we get rid of that odor, we are going to find out about the animal that did that to you!"

Discussing the Story

Undoubtedly the children will recognize this animal. Have they ever seen a skunk? Describe it. Pass around pictures showing the four markings of skunks. Which have they seen? What do they all have in common? Share some of the facts from the "Fun Facts to Share" page, especially the warning signal that the skunk gives, and have them practice it.

Integrating This Unit

- The study of skunks can be taught in connection with a unit on nocturnal animals, such as bats, owls, and raccoons. Have a "nighttime" day in your classroom when everyone comes dressed for bed. Make headbands depicting the various nocturnal animals. Keep the lights off, the shades drawn, and provide flashlights if needed. Pop popcorn and read stories about these animals.

- This unit lends itself to a study of other familiar backyard animals (squirrels, rabbits). Combine it with a camping unit in your dramatic play area as described in the chapter on bears.

- Include this unit when you are exploring the sense of smell.

- Link this unit with a creative arts lesson where the children imagine an animal with a peculiar defense and describe it and its warning signals. They can write an account, draw or model it, and act out the warning.

Interactive Display for Skunks

Choose from the following:
- Picture of Russell
- Several pictures of the four kinds of skunks
- Pieces of black and white faux fur sewn together
- A diorama of a stuffed skunk
- Plastic, rubber, or plush toy skunk
- Models of the other animals in the mustelid family (mink, otter, weasel, and ferret)
- A selection of rigid materials (pencil, bolt, plastic peg, wood block) and flexible materials (wire toy, wristwatch band, pipe cleaner, rubber spatula) to demonstrate the difference between the flexible backbone of the skunk and the more rigid ones of other animals
- Film containers, each filled with a cotton ball that has been dipped in an essence or oil, including musk scent or oil, lemon extract, peppermint, floral, or vinegar
- A paper plate with models/pictures of a skunk's diet, such as a frog, mouse, snake, or caterpillar
- Fiction and nonfiction books about skunks

Take Home Bag for Skunks

Place one or more of the following items in each child's resealable plastic bag. Send the bag home following the introduction or at the end of the unit.

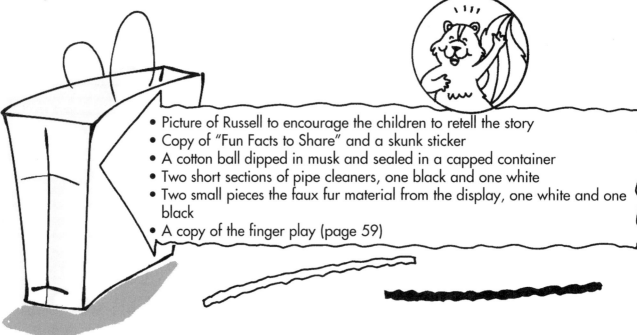

- Picture of Russell to encourage the children to retell the story
- Copy of "Fun Facts to Share" and a skunk sticker
- A cotton ball dipped in musk and sealed in a capped container
- Two short sections of pipe cleaners, one black and one white
- Two small pieces the faux fur material from the display, one white and one black
- A copy of the finger play (page 59)

FUN FACTS to Share

skunk

About Its Body
- Skunks are related to minks, otters, weasels, and ferrets.
- Skunks have a keen sense of smell and hearing, They use these senses while hunting for food.
- Skunks have short legs and sharp claws that they use for digging. They also have long, flexible backbones that allow them to bend their bodies very easily.
- There are four different kinds of skunks: the striped skunk, the spotted skunk, the hog-nosed skunk, and the hooded skunk.
- Baby skunks are called kittens. When they are born, they cannot see or hear, but they do have a thin coat of hair in the same black and white pattern as their parents.

Food
- Skunks eat a wide variety of foods, such as snakes, frogs, mice, and bird and turtle eggs. However, insects such as grasshoppers, caterpillars, crickets, spiders, and grubs are their favorite foods.

Habitat
- Skunks live in dens lined with dried leaves and grasses. They sometimes dig their own dens or use a hollow log for homes. Some may even nest under houses or around barns.

Habits
- To defend themselves against enemies, skunks can release a terrible-smelling liquid called musk.
- Before it sprays, a skunk gives its enemy warnings. First, it stomps with its front feet and rakes the ground with its claws. Then the skunk arches its back, hisses, and raises its tail.
- A skunk is a nocturnal animal.
- Mother skunks teach their babies to hunt, dig for food, and to defend themselves. The kittens usually stay with their mother for six months.

Activities for Skunks

- Read the humorous book *Big Dog and Little Dog Making a Mistake* by Dav Pilkey (Red Wagon, 1999) and then pass around the various film containers containing different scents. Label each container with a letter, numeral, or set of dots. Which smells the most like a skunk? Make a list of all of the words that the children use to describe each odor. Classify the smells into good/bad or strong/delicate.

- Observe any models and/or pictures of skunks and other mustelids. Explain to the children that the skunk has a flexible backbone unlike the rigid backbones of many other animals. During group time, show some of the objects provided in the interactive display and have the children sort them. Have them make their own bodies flexible and then rigid. Invite them to find classroom items that are flexible or rigid. Compare and contrast the skunk with other mustelids.

- Talk about foods that a skunk may eat. Give each child the opportunity to examine the plate containing a skunk's typical diet. What observations can they make? Where do they think skunks might find their food? Make a list of all of their suggestions.

- Take your class for a walk to gather leaves and soft grasses for a skunk den. Have the children place this in a wire bowl or basket. Add a skunk puppet or stuffed toy to the basket. Keep your skunk and her den in the display area.

- Demonstrate how a skunk protects itself. Using a skunk puppet and a spray bottle filled with scented water, demonstrate the three steps that a skunk takes when danger is imminent: stomping its feet and raking the ground with its claws, arching its back and raising its tail, and spraying.

- Move like a skunk. Have the children practice making their bodies flexible and rigid. Play some music. Instruct the children to walk around while the music is playing in a very loose, free, and flexible manner. When the music stops, they are to stop, drop to all fours, stomp their feet, claw the ground, arch their backs, hiss, and become as rigid as possible.

- Identify different scents. Saturate several cotton balls with common scents (lemon oil/extract, vanilla, peppermint, coffee, tea, and cinnamon). Seal the cotton balls in individual plastic film canisters. Make a large hole in each lid. Ask your group to form a circle and pass the canisters around the group. Can the children guess the scents?

- Removing odors from material is sometimes difficult. Saturate a large piece of material with a strong musk scent. Cut the material into several smaller pieces and allow the children to smell them. Ask the children for suggestions of how to remove the scent from the material. Try suggestions that sound reasonable. Some ideas: soak it in tomato juice, a solution of baking soda and water, common household cleaning solution. Check the results. What worked well?

What didn't? Make a chart of your results. Assign the group to ask at home or read about the removal of scents from pets and/or material and report back to the class on methods that work.

- Play "The Skunk and Enemy Game." This game needs to be played outdoors on a warm day. You will need several small spray bottles filled with water. One child is selected to be the skunk and is given one of the bottles. He/She stands between the "enemies" and the safety line. The "enemies" line up facing the "skunk." When the "skunk" stomps its feet, claws the ground, and hisses at the "enemies," the enemies try to reach the safety line before being sprayed by the "skunk." Those sprayed now become "skunks" and are given bottles. Play the game several times, changing the type of enemy each time (fox, bobcat, and owl).

- Try this finger play with your group:
    Out in the backyard (*Put hand to the forehead, as if peering.*)
    Something made me blink. (*Exaggerate blinking.*)
    It was black with a white stripe (*Move pointer finger in a hill motion.*)
    And, boy, did it STINK! (*Wave hand in front of nose.*)

    I pinched my nose (*Pinch nose.*)
    Because it STUNK. (*Say slowly with nose still pinched.*)
    Stay away from me, (*Wag finger.*)
    You black and white skunk! (*Place hands on hips.*)

- Show photographs of four kinds of skunks. Copy and cut out two skunk shapes (see pattern page 61) out of black construction paper for each student. Using white chalk, have them make the white markings of two different skunks.

IF19108 *Super Science Themes*

Introducing Whales

Young children have a natural fascination for very large animals, as evidenced by their love affair with dinosaurs. Whales, too, will capture their imaginations with their bold dimensions, intriguing habits, and intelligent, gentle natures.

Suggested Visuals

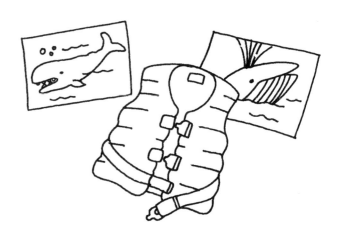

- Picture of Russell
- Full-color pictures of whales
- Life jacket
- Plastic and/or rubber models of whales
- Chart paper and a marker

 **Telling the Story**

Gather the children together for a story time. Bring the items listed above with you. Keep all but the life jacket covered. Before you begin telling the story, show the children the life jacket and ask them where they think you and Russell went on an adventure. Tell this story in your own words.

Over the weekend, it was so beautiful that my neighbors invited me for a ride on their new boat. I said that I really couldn't leave Russell alone for such a long time. They said Russell was invited, too. I was very excited about the boat ride, and Russell was too, at least I thought so. But when we arrived at the marina where the boat was docked, I realized that it wasn't excitement. It was fear. Russell loves an adventure, but sometimes he becomes frightened, too.

I could tell that Russell was very frightened. He was walking in his stutter walk. It looks and sounds like this. (*Demonstrate by making three slow rhythmic slaps on your thighs and then pull your upper body back as you make a frightened expression. Ask your students to try it.*) Russell's tail had dropped between his legs. It no longer wagged with anticipation. With lots of encouragement, Russell finally jumped on board so we could take off on the boat trip.

Then we had another surprise. My neighbor, who was the captain of the boat, handed me a life jacket like this one (*Hold up the life jacket.*) and another smaller one with no armholes for Russell. I didn't know they made life jackets for dogs, did you? Mine snapped on like this (*Demonstrate.*) and Russell's went around his belly and snapped on his underside. (*Take some time to discuss a few rules for safe boating. Why should people and animals wear life jackets on boats?*) When we were all ready, the captain patted Russell's head and said, "Everyone is safe on my boat, Russell." He started the motor and guided the boat toward the ocean water.

At first, Russell sulked under a seat. (*What is sulking? Have you ever sulked?*) But then curiosity got the best of him and he sat up to enjoy the beautiful breeze and the mist of the ocean on his nose. Pretty soon, we could see that some boats had stopped ahead, right there in the ocean. Everyone was looking at something in the water. Our captain slowed down and pulled up beside the other boats. Russell led us to the edge of the boat. While we were standing gazing at the ocean, a huge wide tail thrust itself out of the water. It slapped the water, making a very loud sound (*Make a loud slapping sound.*) and then slid back under the water. It was gone as quickly as it had appeared. Russell was so excited! He was yipping and yapping and wagging his tail as fast as he could when it happened again and again. I said, "As soon as we get back home we're going to hustle, Russell, to the library. We need facts about an ocean animal with a huge tail that goes slap, slap." (*Make two loud slapping sounds.*)

Discussing the Story

Ask your students to guess what kind of animal Russell and the group saw from the boat. Divide a large piece of chart paper into two columns and write down their guesses in one column. Now uncover the pictures and or models of the whales and pass them around the group. Does anybody know what it is called? Write down the children's answers in the second column. Take some time to compare the answers in the two columns.

While the children are examining the materials, ask them to share information they know about whales. Share some of the facts from the "Fun Facts to Share" page. Ask if anyone has seen a whale. Where?

Integrating This Unit

• Use this unit in conjunction with a beach unit. Study several types of marine/beach life.

• Have a beach day/week in your classroom. Set a chair on a platform to be a lifeguard stand. Borrow a small pool and place some rubber or plastic sea creatures in it. Supply the group with beach toys and any other props that you feel appropriate, such as life jackets, whistles, and sunglasses. Have the children bring their bathing suits to school.

• Continue your studies by comparing whales to other marine mammals, such as dolphins and seals.

Interactive Display for Whales

Choose from the following:
- Picture of Russell
- Pictures of various whales, especially the blue whale, sperm whale, humpback whale, grey whale, orca (killer) whale, and beluga whale
- Plastic/rubber models of different whales
- Materials to demonstrate how baleen whales catch their food, for example, sieves, fine-toothed combs, and sifters
- Piece of yarn 9 ft. (2.7 m) long, representing the length of the smallest whale
- Piece of yarn 110 ft. (33.5 m) long, representing the longest whale
- Recordings of whale songs
- Large clear plastic container filled with saltwater, a drop of blue food coloring, plastic plants, gravel, small plastic models of fish, sharks, porpoises, sea turtles and whales to represent ocean life
- Picture of a toothed whale, noting the main parts (eye teeth, blowhole, ear, flipper, dorsal fin, and flukes)
- "Ocean in a Bottle" (see Hermit Crab unit)
- Fiction and nonfiction books about whales

Take Home Bag for Whales

Place one or more of the following items in each child's resealable plastic bag. Send the bag home following the introduction or at the end of the unit.

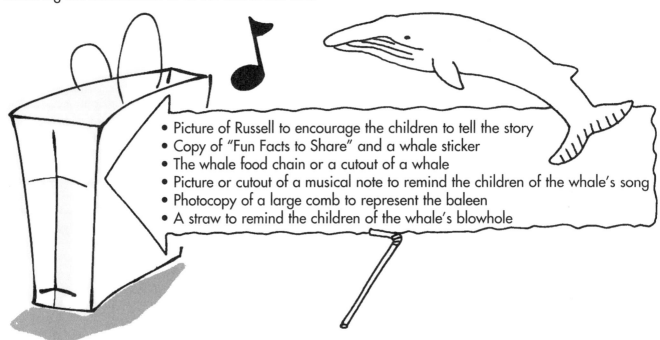

- Picture of Russell to encourage the children to tell the story
- Copy of "Fun Facts to Share" and a whale sticker
- The whale food chain or a cutout of a whale
- Picture or cutout of a musical note to remind the children of the whale's song
- Photocopy of a large comb to represent the baleen
- A straw to remind the children of the whale's blowhole

FUN FACTS to Share

whale

About Its Body
- There are two main types of whales: the toothed whale and the baleen whale.
- Whales cannot breathe underwater like fish, but they can hold their breath for long periods of time—some up to an hour. They breathe air at the surface through a blowhole.
- Mother whales nurse their babies, called calves.

Food
- Toothed whales use their teeth to catch fish, squid, sea birds, and other marine mammals. They swallow them whole.
- Baleen whales have sieve-like structures, called baleens, that catch huge amounts of krill and small fish to eat. The whale uses its tongue to scrape the fish from the baleen. Baleen is make of keratin, the same material as in our fingernails.

Habitat
- Whales are mammals that live in ocean water.

Habits
- The whale swims by moving its tail, called a fluke, up and down.
- Some whales jump high out of the water, even twirling and slapping the water on the way down. This is called breaching.
- Whales make sounds that are known as their songs. Some whales use their songs for echolocation, to attract mates, or to care for their calves.
- The biggest animal that ever lived on the Earth is the blue whale (bigger than the dinosaurs). The blue whale can grow up to 100 feet (30 meters) long and can weigh up to 300,000 lbs. (135 metric tons), which is approximately the weight of 35 elephants.

Activities for Whales

- Compare the lengths of whales. Have students hold up and stretch out the pieces of yarn in the Interactive Display, depicting the longest and shortest whales. Have the children describe the two lengths of yarn in nonstandard terms of measurement. For example, "the shortest whale is as long as two of our tables." The longest whale is as long as the hallway from our door to Mrs. Jones's desk.

- Play a riddle game with your students to reinforce the difference between fish and whales. Give each child a cutout shape of a fish and a whale and have them raise the correct cutout in the air to answer each riddle. Use the following riddles or make up some of your own.

    I breathe through my gills. What am I?

    I swim by moving my fluke up and down. What am I?

    I travel in a group called a pod. What am I?

    I lay eggs. What am I?

    I have scales. What am I?

    After my baby is born, I nurse it with my milk. What am I?

    I travel in a school. What am I?

    I breathe air through a blowhole into my lungs. What am I?

    I move my tail from side to side to swim. What am I?

    I can hold my breath for a long time. What am I?

    I have many enemies in the ocean. What am I?

    I can live in freshwater or saltwater. What am I?

    I catch my food in a filter called a baleen. What am I?

- Sift out objects like the baleen whale. Set out a clear plastic tub filled half full with water, to which gravel has been added. Explain how the baleen whale strains his food from the water using baleen. Pass out some common items that would work in a similar way to a baleen, such as fine-toothed combs, sieves, or any other kind of filter, to see what students can "catch" with their makeshift baleen. Try adding a variety of smaller and larger items to the water. What things are easy to catch? What things are difficult?

- Sing the song "Toothed Whale Hokey Pokey" with your class. Use the following verses:

    Put their teeth in. . .

    Put their blowhole in. . . (*Place a fist on top of head and put head in.*)

    Put one flipper in. . . (*Have arm folded at elbow.*)

    Put the other flipper in. . . (*Have opposite arm folded at elbow.*)

    Put the dorsal fin in. . . (*Hands pressed together in the middle of the back.*)

    Put the fluke in. . . (*Hands together and spread outward in back, below the waist.*)

- Teach about the whale food chain by using a piece of string or yarn. Provide each child with a enlarged copy (see pattern on page 69) of plankton or a small fish, a larger fish, a shark, and a toothed whale. Punch a hole in each cutout and have the children decorate it. Give each child an 18 in. (46 cm) piece of string or yarn with a knot at one end and have them thread the cutouts on the string/yarn in the correct order (smallest to largest). Knot the other end of the string to keep the cutouts from slipping off. Have the children stretch out their food chain, arranging all the cutouts an equal distance apart. Now have the children slide the large fish over the small fish/plankton, the shark over the fish, and whale over the shark to demonstrate how this food chain works. Hang the food chains up or save them for the Take Home Bag.

- Make a classroom mural of a whale pod. Take a large piece of white butcher paper and have the children cover it with various shades of purple and blue using small rollers or sponges. Provide each child with a whale cutout (page 68) and have them color and glue it to the mural. The child can also draw or paint whales directly on the mural.

- Make an "ocean in a bottle" (directions in the Hermit Crab unit) but add a whale by blowing up a water-balloon sized balloon. Let out most of the air and tie it about a third of the way up. Squeeze the balloon into the bottle. Replace the cap and tape it securely.

- Play actual recordings of whale songs for your group. If possible, demonstrate high, low, fast, and short sounds on various musical instruments. Have the children stand up for high sounds and squat down for the low ones. Play some notes sharply and draw out others. Have the children move appropriately. Encourage each child to make up a whale song of high, low, fast, and short sounds, using "oohs" and "aahs" or whatever sounds they like. Tape their songs and then play them back. Have the children try to identify the singer of each song and then try to mimic the song.

- Make a whale-shaped snack. Give each child two refrigerated biscuits and have him create a snack. Shape the first biscuit into a basic whale shape. Use the second biscuit to add the dorsal fin, the flippers, and the flukes. A blowhole can be carved out with a toothpick. Use new paintbrushes for painting the whales with food coloring and bake according to the directions on the package. Serve with butter or jam.

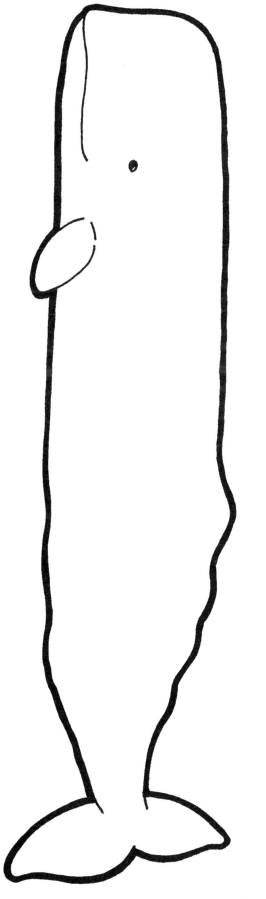

Introducing Owls

Because owls are night creatures, children's association with them is generally through stories and videos. Children view owls as either wise animals like Owl in *Winnie the Pooh* or as spooky creatures as in many Halloween stories. This unit will provide valuable information on the owl's unique position in the bird kingdom and will dispel both myths.

Suggested Visuals

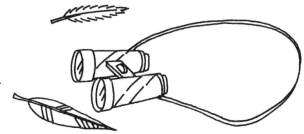

- Picture of Russell
- Soft, fluffy feathers and a stiff, pointed feather
- Pictures of various species of owls
- Binoculars

 **Telling the Story**

Gather your students together for a story time. Bring one or more items from the Interactive Display but keep them covered. Hold up the picture of Russell and ask the children what they remember about Russell. Tell this story in your own words.

The other day after I finished my chores, I asked Russell if he wanted to take a ride in the car to the State Park where we could go for a hike. Russell loves the car. (*Ask the children about their dogs. Do they like to ride in the car?*) He ran as fast as he could (*Demonstrate fast running on knees.*) and sat down next to the car door. I opened the door and spread an old towel over the seat because sometimes Russell gets muddy when we walk in the woods. Russell jumped in. Guess where Russell sat? He sat right up front in the passenger seat. He's very quiet and looked straight ahead until we were on the road.

When we arrived at the park, Russell was very excited. He loved to snoop. We had been walking on the path for awhile when Russell ran ahead of me (*Pat hands on knees to make running sound.*) and was sniffing the ground under a large tree. Suddenly he sneezed five times in a row. (*Have the children pretend to sneeze five times in a row.*) We started walking again, but Russell kept looking back. Finally, he ran back to the exact same spot, and then put his nose near the ground. And what do you think happened? Russell sneezed five more times!

I bent down to see what I could see, and I found what was tickling Russell's nose. There on the ground were some very soft and fluffy feathers. I went to pick them up when I also spotted a long pointed feather. "Hustle, Russell," I said. "Let's find out what kind of bird feathers made you sneeze."

Discussing the Story

Ask the children what animal they think it could be? Make a list of all of their responses. Pass around the fluffy feathers and the pointed feathers. Are there any birds that they can now eliminate? Bring out the binoculars and tell them that they are a clue. Are there any more birds that they can eliminate? Pass the pictures of owls around the group. Ask, "What do you know about owls? What would you like to learn about owls?"

As the children continue to look at the materials, share some facts about owls from the "Fun Facts to Share" page. Ask for questions. If you cannot answer them, look up the answers with the children. Older students will be ready for longer and more detailed explanations and to find information on their own.

Integrating This Unit

- Combine the study of owls with other "Halloween" animals, such as the bat and the spider. Why do the children think that these animals are associated with Halloween? Are they really scary? Discuss and dispel the myths surrounding bats and owls.

- Include the study of owls with other nocturnal animals. Plan a "nighttime" day in your classroom as described in the chapter on skunks.

- Complete a comprehensive unit on birds and include owls as one topic.

- Set up a farm/barnyard in your dramatic play area by bringing in bales of hay, a wheelbarrow, tractor riding toy, rocking horse, stuffed animals, straw hats, and bandanas. Be sure to include a barn owl.

Interactive Display for Owls

Choose from the following:
- Several color pictures of various kinds of owls
- Binoculars to demonstrate an owl's vision
- Two pieces of colorful yarn taped on a flat surface in your display area, representing the wingspan of the pygmy owl (16.2 in. or 32 cm) and the wingspan of the eagle owl (6.6 ft. or 2 m).
- Plastic or rubber models of owls
- A diorama or stuffed owl
- A collection of soft, fluffy feathers and stiff, pointed feathers to show the two different types of owl feathers
- Pictures or models of small animals that owls hunt, such as birds and mice
- Pictures or models of other kinds of birds that show the vast differences in birds
- Optional: A live display of mice, the owl's most common prey
- Fiction and nonfiction books about owls

Take Home Bag for Owls

Place one or more of the following items in each child's resealable plastic bag. Send the bag home following the introduction or at the end of the unit.

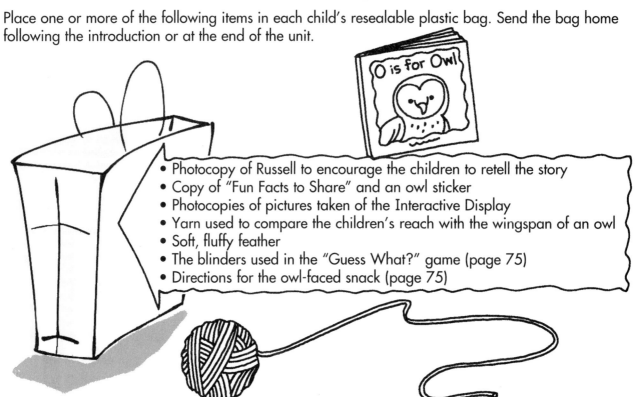

- Photocopy of Russell to encourage the children to retell the story
- Copy of "Fun Facts to Share" and an owl sticker
- Photocopies of pictures taken of the Interactive Display
- Yarn used to compare the children's reach with the wingspan of an owl
- Soft, fluffy feather
- The blinders used in the "Guess What?" game (page 75)
- Directions for the owl-faced snack (page 75)

FUN FACTS to Share

owl

About Its Body

- Many owls also have feathers sticking up on their heads. They look like ears. They are called ear tufts.
- Most birds have eyes on the sides of their heads, but owls have eyes that face forward. This gives them vision that is like wearing binoculars.
- Owls have small bodies, but they have many very thick, soft feathers. Their soft feathers make no sound when they fly. This makes it easier to sneak up on prey.

Food

- Owls feed on rabbits, mice, squirrels, rats, and shrews. Some owls will hunt insects and small birds.

Habitat

- Owls live in all parts of the world. Most owls live in wooded areas, but some owls live in the cold tundra. Some live in tropical jungles and some in the desert.

Habits

- Most owls are nocturnal birds. They sleep during the day and come out at night to hunt small prey.
- Owls cannot move their eyes within their sockets, so they have to move their heads to see in different directions. They can move their heads almost all the way around.
- Owls have claws called talons (TAL-uns) that are dangerous weapons. The talons make it easy for owls to grab their prey.

Activities for Owls

- Examine an owl (pictures or model). Record the children's observations about its features. Look closely at all of the sensory features. What do owls have in common with other familiar birds? What is different?

- Fill a container with small soft feathers and pass it around the group. Have the children feel the feathers. Make a list of adjectives that describe the feathers. Explain that small soft feathers cover most of the owl's body. On the count of three, have one of the children let the feathers fall to the ground. What observations do the children make?

- Examine long, pointed feathers and talk about how this kind of feather is also on an owl's body. Make a list of all of the students' observations and descriptive words. Discuss why this kind of feather is needed on the owl's body.

- Use binoculars to view plants and animals. Provide several pairs of binoculars for the children to use. Explain that binocular vision mimics an owl's vision. Ask the children: How is this different from our vision? Would they like to have binocular vision? Why or why not? How would this vision help an owl? Play a game where one child finds a small object and puts it somewhere across the room, giving some clues as to its location. Have another child look for that object with the binoculars.

- Have the children sort pictures of nocturnal and diurnal animals. Locate two large shoebox lids. Draw a large sun at the top of one box lid and a moon at the top of the other lid. Laminate pictures of nocturnal animals (skunk, raccoon, bat, owl, mouse) and animals that are active during daytime. (See pattern page 77 for some animal pictures to start the collection.) Introduce the animals and then have the children sort the pictures accordingly.

- Choosing a meal for an owl. Place a plastic dinner plate and a small basket filled with items or pictures such as: small bird, plastic mouse, flower, carrot, plastic spider, plastic insects, and nuts. Have the children take turns choosing a good meal for an owl by placing "owl food" on the plate. Afterward, hold up each item and ask the children if this is something an owl would like.

- Compare sizes. Have the child extend his arms and then cut a piece of yarn that length. Have the children compare their pieces of yarn with the colored tape lengths in the Interactive Display area. Save the yarn for the Take Home Bag.

- Investigate how owls use their talons to catch and hold their food. To better understand what this is like, have the children try picking up a variety of small classroom objects with a clamp.

- Paint with feathers. Have the children paint pictures using small fluffy feathers and stiff, pointed feathers.

- Have the children make blinders and wear them to see what it is like to have no peripheral vision. Ask the children to bring baseball caps from home. Tape some tag board pieces that they have decorated to the sides of the brims to block their peripheral vision. Now play a game called "Guess What?" Have the child wear the blinders while you hold an object near the side of her head. Ask the child to identify the object without moving her head. Now have the child take off the blinders and repeat the exercise.

- Read aloud the book *Fly by Night* by June Crebbin (Candlewick Press, 1993). Together make a class list of things for which it is difficult to wait.

- Make an owl-faced snack. Place a piece of cheese on top of a rice cake. Add two slices of pepperoni with olive slices in their centers for eyes and a triangular cracker for a beak. Heat the snack in a microwave or toaster oven to melt the cheese slightly.

- Play a circle game called "Whooo's missing, Mr./Ms. Owl?" One child is Mr. Owl and sits in the middle of the circle, covering his eyes. Choose another child to leave the circle and hide in another area of the room. When the child is hidden, the children in the circle say, "Whoooo's missing, Mr. Owl?" Mr. Owl then opens his eyes and makes two guesses to identify who is missing. The group answers, "Yes (No), Mr. Owl." The child who was hiding then gets to be Mr./Ms. Owl.

- Make a pine cone owl. You will need one large and one small pine cone for each child. Also provide feathers, glue, wiggly craft eyes, and paper triangles for beaks. Use the large pine cone as the main part of the owl's body and glue on the smaller one for the owl's head (the bottom of the large pine cone). Affix the eyes and beak. Dip the stem of each feather in the glue and poke it into the pine cone.

raccoon

mouse

barn owl

robin

rabbit

turtle

Introducing Penguins

Penguins are one of the most unusual birds in existence. Their comical appearance and walk appeal to children who are often asked to imitate them in movement classes.

Suggested Visuals

- Picture of Russell
- Full-color pictures of several species of penguins
- Penguin puppet
- Globe or world map

Telling the Story

Gather the children together for a story time. Bring one or more items from the Interactive Display but keep them covered. Hold up the picture of Russell and ask the children what they remember about Russell. Tell this story in your own words.

Last weekend, Russell and I had quite an adventure. You know that Russell and I like to roam in the woods or near lakes and streams where things are pretty quiet. Last week, we were invited to visit our friends in the city and decided to go. I tried to explain to Russell that things would be very different in the city. He'd have to stay on his leash and walk at a nice even pace as we strolled with our friends. Russell shook his head in agreement, wagged his tail, and even showed me how polite he would act.

Our friends lived on the eleventh floor in a big apartment building. They suggested that we should all go for a walk, so we piled into the elevator (*Russell had never been on an elevator before.*) and headed down to first floor. Soon we were outside and walking in the brisk air. It was strange to walk on big city streets with so many people and so many other dogs, but Russell was doing just fine, walking his finest walk. (*Pat hands on thighs in very dignified way.*) Then out of nowhere came a barrage of emergency vehicles with their sirens blasting like this. (*Have children help you make loud emergency sounds.*) We had turned to watch the commotion when Russell bolted through the crowd at his fastest pace. (*Pat thighs furiously with hands.*) Russell hates sirens.

"There's a park nearby," my friend had said, "and Russell's probably heading there. It is calmer, actually very quiet, there. In fact, there's a very nice zoo in that park." What? A zoo! You know how curious Russell is! I was sure his great sniffer would lead him right there, so I ran as fast as I could to the entrance. (*Clap hands on knees quickly.*) Once inside, I jogged past the lions, tigers, elephants, and monkeys, and then I followed some zoo attendants who were running toward the bird house. There was Russell sitting (*Show begging position.*) as quiet as could be, looking at about twenty black and white birds that were standing on ice looking back at him.

"Hustle, Russell," I said. "A zoo is no place for a dog! We'll find out about those birds, if they are birds, when we get out of here!"

Discussing the Story

Ask the children if they know what Russell was looking at in the birdhouse. Why would we be confused about whether this animal was a bird or a sea creature? Pass around any picture/models that you have brought to the story time. Ask the children: What do you know about penguins? Where have you seen them at other times? Present the map or globe. Place a small paper arrow on your city and another arrow pointing down at the Southern Hemisphere where penguins live. Compile a list of questions that the children have about penguins. Share some facts about penguins from the "Fun Facts to Share" page.

Integrating This Unit

- Combine this unit with a unit on winter. Collect clothing for the winter season and talk about their insulating properties. How do penguins keep warm in such frigid temperatures?

- Study different kinds of birds. On butcher paper, have the children draw pictures of several different kinds of environments, such as the rain forest, grassland, desert, tundra, and Antarctica. Cut out pictures of animals and glue them onto the appropriate scene.

- Create an interesting unit on confusing species of animals. Why do some people think that penguins are sea creatures, that spiders are insects, that bats are birds, and that whales are fish?

79

Interactive Display for Penguins

Choose from the following:

- Picture of Russell
- Several pictures of various kinds of penguins
- Models of or stuffed penguins
- A globe with arrows pointing to your location and to the Southern Hemisphere
- Pieces of string to indicate the heights of the largest and smallest penguins
- Recordings of penguin sounds
- Collection of light and dark fabrics (Have the children sort them. Place them in the sun to see if the children can tell which absorbs more heat.)
- An outdoor thermometer for the children to observe for several days (Record the indoor temperature for several days and then take the thermometer outside and record the outdoor temperature for several days as well.)
- Make a huge ice cube by freezing colored water in a large plastic container. Provide small plastic penguins that the children can "toboggan" on the ice.
- Arrange a display of hollow and dense objects such as a pipe and a dowel, a walnut and a hollowed nut, a small wooden box and a block, and a brick and a hollow cardboard brick.
- Fiction and nonfiction books about penguins

Take Home Bag for Penguins

Place one or more of the following items in each child's resealable plastic bag. Send the bag home following the introduction or at the end of the unit.

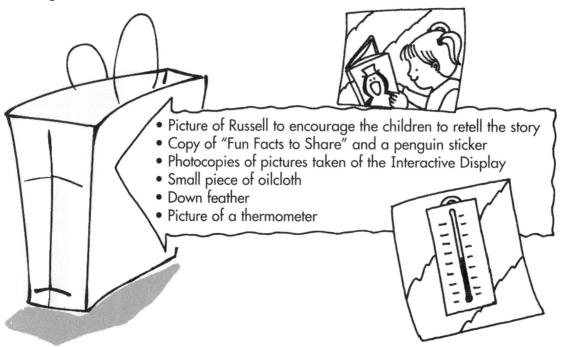

- Picture of Russell to encourage the children to retell the story
- Copy of "Fun Facts to Share" and a penguin sticker
- Photocopies of pictures taken of the Interactive Display
- Small piece of oilcloth
- Down feather
- Picture of a thermometer

FUN FACTS to Share

penguin

About Its Body
- Like all birds, penguins have feathers and lay eggs.
- Penguins walk on their flat feet. Some waddle while others walk straight.
- When penguins swim, their wings act as flippers while their feet are used for steering.
- Penguins have small, dense outside feathers. They are covered with oil that makes them waterproof.

Food
- Penguins eat crabs, squid, fish, and very small animals called krill.
- Adult penguins will leave for long periods of time looking for food and eating.

Habitat
- All wild penguins live south of the equator in the Southern Hemisphere. Many live in areas with extremely cold temperatures, such as Antarctica.

Habits
- Penguins spend much of their time swimming and diving for food.
- Penguins cannot breathe underwater. Some can hold their breath for as long as 20 minutes.
- All penguins communicate by making sounds such as braying, whistling, trilling, screaming, and trumpeting.
- When penguins tire of walking, they lie on their bellies and slide on the ice. This is called tobogganing.
- When the air temperature is extremely cold, the penguin chicks and adult penguins will huddle together. The penguins in the hot interior will make their way to the outside of the huddle, giving all of the penguins a turn at being on the outside, the inside, and in the center of the group.

Activities for Penguins

- Examine a penguin (pictures, model). Record the children's observations. Talk about where they may have watched penguins swim, walk, and eat food. Ask the children: What do penguins have in common with other familiar birds? How is it that a penguin can be a bird and not fly?

- Talk about the concepts of hollow and dense with the children. Explain how most birds have hollow bones and that the penguin has solid bones. Pass the hollow and dense objects around the group and ask what they notice. How would dense bones help a penguin?

- Play an audiotape of penguin sounds. Ask the children to describe the sounds. For what reasons do they think penguins need to make sounds?

- Investigate the importance of oil on feathers. Help the children understand how the oil on the penguin's feathers makes them waterproof. Give each child a dessert-size paper plate and a pipe cleaner. Pass around a small container of vegetable oil and have each child put a teaspoon (3 mL) of oil on its plate. Next have them dip their pipe cleaner into a container of water and drop it onto the oil. What happens to the water?

- Test fabrics/materials to learn which ones are water repellent. Fill a small basket with scraps of fabric and other materials including cotton, wool, oilcloth, pieces of yarn, and vinyl. Set out a dishpan of water. Have the child choose an item, predict whether the item will be waterproof or not, and dip it into the water. Did any fabrics or items fool the children?

- Learn about the concept of insulation. Do the following experiment with the children. Set out a large bowl of ice water and have each child dip one hand into it. How does it feel? Now have the child put on a rubber glove and then test the water. Did that change anything? Finally, fill a baggie with a very thick layer of vegetable shortening that covers the bottom and both sides. Explain that the vegetable shortening is fat and that penguins have a very thick layer of fat under their skin called blubber. Have the child put her rubber-gloved hand into the middle of the baggie and submerge the hand into the ice water. What effect does the blubber have?

- Gather hollow and dense items from the interactive display and have the children weigh them. Make a classroom chart recording the results.

- Learn how to read a simple thermometer. Most penguins live in cold temperatures. Make thermometers with the children. Cut pieces of poster board 3 in. by 8 in. (8 cm x 28 cm). With a hobby/craft knife, cut a ½ in. (13 mm) slit, 1½ in. (38 mm) from each of the long ends. Give each child an 11 in. (28 cm) piece of ⅜ in. (10 mm) elastic. With a red marker, have them color the bottom half of the elastic red. Then thread the elastic into each end. Secure the two ends together in the back with duct tape. If the children are old enough, have them write the numbers onto the thermometer, using as many or as few numbers as you wish. Then play a game of finding a given temperature on the thermometer.

- Gather the children together to make a penguin huddle. Have a core group of three to five children in the center. Have them decide on their favorite penguin sound and at regular intervals, when they make that sound, they will move outward as the other penguins move gradually inward until the core group is on the outside. Take turns having the next interior group decide on their call. How did they feel when they were in different parts of the huddle?

- Provide penguin stamps, ink pads, and watercolor paints in the art center. Invite the children to paint Antarctic winter scenes with watercolor paints and then stamp a penguin colony onto each painting.

- How long is 20 minutes? Remind the children of the fact that a penguin cannot breathe underwater, but that it can hold its breath for up to 20 minutes. Set a timer for 20 minutes and put it inside of a penguin puppet. Notice how long this is. Reset the timer for 30 seconds and have the students try to hold their breath for that long.

- Perform the following finger play.
    I'm an emperor penguin dad (*Point to chest with thumb.*)
    And I like the ice and snow. (*Hands crossed over chest, shivering.*)
    I take care of my chick egg (*Cup hands.*)
    It goes everywhere I go. (*Walk with fingers.*)

    I have a special place (*Hands held together over heart.*)
    To cover my baby sweet. (*Make hands into cradle and rock.*)
    It's a warm, snuggly spot (*Hands held over cheeks.*)
    On the top of my feet! (*Surprised expression. Point to feet.*)

- Walk like penguins on a path. Make the path by securing pieces of masking tape on the floor to designate a short route for your classroom penguins to walk. Explain that penguins have very short legs and that is why so many penguins waddle when they walk. Have the children get on their knees with their arms at their sides and their hands pointing slightly out. Have them walk the line. When they get to the end of the path, have the children decide if they were waddlers or not. Give each child a penguin cutout (see page 85) to color. Have each child glue it onto a graph of waddlers and straight walkers.

Emperor Penguin

Introducing Salmon

Young children will stand or sit for long periods of time in front of an aquarium, watching fish glide smoothly through the water. No matter if the children have or have not had opportunities to observe different kinds of fish, they will be intrigued with the migrating habits of the salmon.

Suggested Visuals

- Picture of Russell
- Pictures of several types of salmon and the streams where they spawn
- Pictures of a dam
- Stuffed salmon or a model of a salmon
- Fishing rod and reel

Telling the Story

Gather the children together for a story time. Bring one or more items from the Interactive Display but keep them covered. Hold up the picture of Russell and ask the children what they remember about Russell. Tell this story in your own words.

There is a large dam on a river that is a short drive from my house. Have you ever seen a dam? Have you built a dam in a muddy place to block a tiny stream of water? (*Allow the children some time to share their knowledge of dams with the group. Show a picture of a dam and briefly explain its purpose.*) I have been very curious about this dam and wanted to see it for a long time. Last Saturday, Russell and I drove over to see the dam. Russell must have been curious about the dam, too, because when I told him we were going to see it, he could hardly wait to get into the car. He ran as fast as he could to the car and hopped into the front seat.

When we arrived at the dam, we parked our car in the parking lot along the river. It was a beautiful day with bright sunshine and large puffy clouds in the sky. Russell was very excited as we walked down the path toward the dam. Seeing someone up ahead of us on the path, he ran toward him. (*Clap your hands on your thighs to create a running rhythm and encourage the children to join it.*) Although I don't run as quickly as Russell, I sprinted after him. (*Clap your hands on your thighs in a slower running rhythm.*) When I caught up with Russell, he was standing near a fisherman who was holding a long fishing rod and reel like this one. (*Show the rod and reel.*) Russell had never seen anyone fishing before and so we stood there quietly and watched. As we were standing there, we saw some beautiful silver fish leaping high into the air to get over some big rocks that were in the river. One of the fish must have made a mistake because it leapt so high that it landed on the bank of the river right near Russell's feet. I was so surprised that I jumped backwards and so did Russell. Then Russell, who is usually scared of new things, did something very brave. He picked up the fish very gently in his mouth, ran over to the edge of the river, and dropped the fish back into the water where it quickly swam away. What a

86

hero Russell was! I clapped for Russell because I was so proud of him, and he liked it. (*Clap your hands and encourage the children to join it.*) Then I said, "Hustle, Russell, we need to go to the library and find out about a beautiful silver fish that can leap like that."

Discussing the Story

Ask the children if they know what kind of fish it might be. Make a list of their responses. Pass around any picture/models that you have brought to the story time. If none of the students have come up with the name "salmon," tell the group the name of the fish and share with them some characteristics of salmon from the "Fun Facts to Share" page. Have any of them ever heard of this fish? What have they heard?

Integrating This Unit

- Combine this unit with one on camping or outdoor sports. Set up a "campsite" in your room. To make a stream, place a blue plastic tarp or some blue cellophane on the floor. Add a few rocks of various sizes. Trace and cut out several salmon from construction paper and cover them with clear adhesive plastic. Affix a large metal paper clip near the mouth of each fish and place it in the "stream." Provide your "campers" with fishing rods made from a tree branch or thin dowel rod. Add string with a magnet tied to the end and start fishing.

- Make a study of fresh and saltwater fish. Compare and contrast the two. Where do salmon fit?

- Along with the study of salmon, learn more about dams. Have your students build some simple dams in your sand table. Later, make a study of increasingly complicated structures made from clay and blocks and include fish ladders.

Interactive Display for Salmon

Choose from the following:
- Picture of Russell
- Several pictures of various kinds of salmon
- Pictures of streams, rivers, and oceans where salmon might live
- Pictures of dams
- Stuffed salmon
- Plastic models of salmon
- Fossils of fish
- Magnifying glasses and fish scales that have been dried and cleaned
- Fishing rod, reel, and other fishing paraphernalia for the students to touch and manipulate
- Scale and weights to match the weight of some kinds of salmon
- A string about 11 ft. (3.3 m) long to demonstrate how high a salmon can leap
- A topographical map of the northeastern or northwestern states containing streams where salmon spawn
- Small aquarium with minnows or guppies to observe how they swim and breathe
- Fiction and nonfiction books about salmon

Take Home Bag for Salmon

Place one or more or the following items in each child's resealable plastic bag. Send the bag home following the introduction or at the end of the unit.

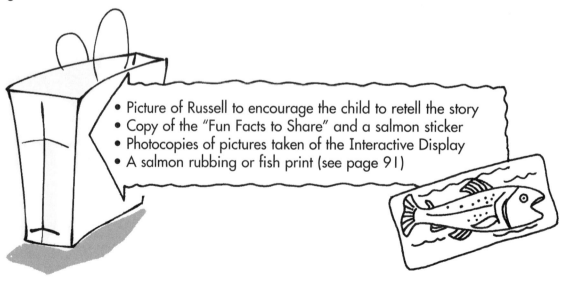

- Picture of Russell to encourage the child to retell the story
- Copy of the "Fun Facts to Share" and a salmon sticker
- Photocopies of pictures taken of the Interactive Display
- A salmon rubbing or fish print (see page 91)

FUN FACTS to Share

salmon

About Its Body
- A salmon has seven fins that all work together to help it swim fast and slow, move up and down, and stop.
- The salmon has a wide field of vision and only things that are very close to its face are difficult for it to see.
- Chinook salmon have long, sleek, muscular bodies. In the ocean their sides are silvery blue, their backs are blue-green, and their bellies are almost white.
- Salmon sleep with their eyes open because they have no eyelids.

Food
- Young salmon eat small sea creatures such as shrimp and tiny organisms called plankton. As they grow, they eat sand eels, small herring, other small fish, squid, and shrimp.

Habitat
- The salmon spends most of its life either in the waters of the Atlantic or the Pacific ocean.

Habits
- Salmon have been known to leap 11 feet (3.3 m) into the air.
- All salmon start their lives in freshwater and migrate to the ocean. They go back to their home streams to spawn.
- Little is known about the salmon's life in the sea. It feeds and grows.
- Some salmon swim more than 2,500 miles (4,000 km) from their home waters.
- Some scientists believe that salmon use the sun by day and the ocean currents to navigate its way back to freshwater. Once in freshwater, the salmon use taste and smell to find the home water.

Activities for Salmon

- Contact your State Department of Natural Resources to find out if someone could speak with your group about fish in your area. He or she should concentrate their talk on the fish, their habits and habitats, and the way nature has changed around them.

- Read the book *The Magic School Bus Goes Up Stream* by Bruce Degan (Scholastic Books, 1997) to your class and have your own class picnic. Toast bagels, spread with cream cheese, and add small slivers of smoked salmon. Cut into bite-sized pieces and enjoy.

- Discuss obstacles that salmon meet on their way back to their home streams. Show several pictures of rapids, waterfalls, dams, and other dangers that salmon may meet as they travel upstream. Plan a challenging outdoor obstacle course with your group. Suggestions for the course: Go up the slide. Step through tires (backward). Climb a wall/fence. Roll up or down a hill. Crawl using only the arms. Climb a rope. Jump down from an age-appropriate height.

- Perform this finger play:
    Down the river and to the sea,
    Swims little salmon wild and free. (*Turn hand sideways and make a swimming motion.*)
    He eats and grows for quite a while, (*Extend fingers, thumb underneath and mimic eating by opening and closing hand.*)
    Then returns to his home, mile after mile. (*Repeat swimming motion.*)

- Play a game called "Do I Eat Salmon?" Locate pictures from magazines and the Internet of several animals that eat salmon, such as gulls, eagles, bears, seals, otters, porpoises, cormorants, eels, and humans. Also find pictures of animals that do not feed on salmon, such as horses, cows, chickens, frogs, and shrimp. Laminate the pictures for durability. Discuss the pictures with the children. Give each child a "yes" and "no" card. Laminate and save them for other similar games. Have a student hold up a picture of an animal as she asks, "Do I eat salmon?" The players hold up either the "yes" or "no" card in answer.

- Scientists, environmentalists, and other groups are tagging and counting salmon to find out more about their habits, numbers, and life cycles. Designate several children to be salmon and others to be researchers. Instruct the "salmon" to "swim" from one selected spot to another as many times as they can during a certain amount of time (say 30 seconds) while the counters record one tally mark for each fish on a piece of paper. Keep track of the time. When the 30 seconds is up, stop and have each of the researchers report on how many fish went by during the 30 seconds.

- Make a salmon rubbing. Photocopy the picture of the salmon on page 92. Squeeze a thin line of glue over all the lines in the picture and then set it aside to dry over night. Tape the glue lined drawing securely to a table. Have the children cover the drawing with a thin sheet of white paper and rub over the white paper with the side of a crayon or chalk. This same rubbing technique can be used with any fish fossils that you are able to obtain from collectors or the lending section of a natural history museum.

- Scientists believe that salmon can smell and/or taste the small differences in the water of various streams and this is how they locate the exact stream that they came from. Have the children try this activity. Divide your group into teams. Each team will be a group of salmon from a different stream. Make stream water for each team by adding a certain flavor to each, such as orange, lemon, vanilla. Allow each team member to taste and smell his/her "water." Have the teams leave the room while you place several samples of the various waters around the room. As the children come back into the room, lead them to each "stream" to taste and smell the water. When they have found the correct "stream," they stay by that water until each member of the team has found his/her "home stream."

- Talk about the salmon's migration habits. Show the children a topographical map of the northwestern or northeastern coastline of North America that contains several streams and creeks where salmon spawn. Ask the children to explain how salmon are able to find their home stream out of all those located on the map. Read the book *The Magic School Bus Goes Upstream* by Joana Cole (Scholastic, 1997).

- Learn about ways to save the salmon population. Find out what some people are doing to increase the salmon population. Read aloud the book *Come Back, Salmon* by Molly Cone (Sierra Club Books for Kids, 1994) to your group.

- Use the string from the Display Center that is 11 ft. (3.4 m) long. Stretch it out and tape it to a wall in an area where your students can leap next to it. Make sure that one end touches the floor. Allow each child to take a turn leaping into the air. Mark on the string with tape approximately how high that child was able to leap. Have each child measure the distance from the floor to his/her mark and compare it to the distance that salmon leap. As a follow up, measure each child. Then have each child compare his/her length to that of a salmon. The Chum is approximately 18 in. (45.7 cm) long.

92

Introducing Sharks

When they think of the ocean, children most often think of sharks and whales. Some very young children already have collections of models of different sharks that they delight in bringing to "Show-and-Tell." Children seem to be most intrigued with the "danger" aspect of sharks and to know little else. While it is true that sharks can be dangerous, attacks are rare. This unit will help children learn about the interesting lives of sharks.

Suggested Visuals

- Picture of Russell
- Pictures and models of sharks
- Coarse sandpaper
- String representing the size of the smallest shark

 **Telling the Story**

Gather the children together for a story time. Bring one or more items from the Interactive Display but keep them covered. Hold up the picture of Russell and ask the children what they remember about Russell. Tell this story in your own words.

Last week Russell and I were riding in the car going to buy dog food when I remembered that Aunt Susan wanted me to stop and see the new exhibit on sharks. Naturally, I thought she meant to include Russell, since you know how interested Russell is in all animals. Russell was so excited. He was wagging his tail as fast as he could (*Wave hand back and forth very fast.*) and whimpering like this. (*Have children make the sound.*) Aunt Susan was there to meet us. Russell bounded out of the car and planted a big, slurpy kiss right on Aunt Susan's cheek. "Sorry, Russell," she said, "no dogs are allowed." Russell was mad. He started yipping and yapping. Aunt Susan's friends were there to take Russell for a walk. He left with his tail hanging between his legs and his head held down low.

Aunt Susan led me inside. Wow! Sharks! First we went into a classroom where we watched a great video on sharks. Then we walked to a large holding tank to see a real nurse shark. Aunt Susan said that if I wanted I could touch the nurse shark. I was a little nervous, but I really wanted to touch a real shark's skin. Was I ever surprised! The shark felt so rough and prickly that I thought I was feeling sandpaper!

When I returned to the car, I expected Russell to be pouting, but he was happy to see me and acted like he had a secret. When we got home, Russell rushed downstairs to our tool room. I was putting away the dog food when he came back with a piece of sandpaper in his mouth and dropped it right on my feet. What was Russell up to? Did he somehow know about the shark? "Hustle, Russell," I said. "I don't have a clue how you could know about the sandpaper, but I do know that you're going to love learning about sharks!"

Discussing the Story

Ask the children to tell what they know about sharks and where they have seen them. Make a list of the names of sharks that they know. Pass the sandpaper around the group and then have the children think of descriptive words. How do most fish feel? (slippery, slimy) Hypothesize about the reason that the shark's skin is different.

As the children continue to look at the materials you have collected, share some facts about sharks from the "Fun Facts to Share" page. Ask for questions. If you cannot answer them, look up the answers with the children. Older students will be ready for longer and more detailed explanations and to find information on their own.

Integrating This Unit

- Combine this unit with the favorite dinosaur unit, since sharks actually precede dinosaurs. Convert a tabletop into a prehistoric environment including both land and sea and plenty of models of sharks and dinosaurs. Why do the children think sharks survived while dinosaurs became extinct?

- Choose several animals, such as the shark, elephant, and alligator, and compare them with their prehistoric ancestors. Pair the children up—one taking the prehistoric and the other the modern counterpart—and have them draw pictures and dictate or write a fact. Compile these into a classroom book.

- Combine this unit with one of animals living in or near the sea, such as sharks, penguins, sea lions, and whales that have made adaptations to help them survive. What adaptations do people make or have they made to survive?

Interactive Display for Sharks

Choose from the following:
- Picture of Russell
- Several pictures of various kinds of sharks
- Rubber or plastic models of sharks
- Two strings—one cut to the length of the shortest shark, the dwarf shark, which is 6.5 in. (17 cm) and one cut to the length of the longest shark, which is the whale shark at 59 ft. (49 m).
- A shark tooth or shark jaw (Note: Display it out of the children's reach.)
- Products made with shark oil (Note: Display them out of the children's reach.)
- Coarse sandpaper
- Set up a shark habitat in the water table or a large plastic container with your students (Research the topic to find suitable items for the display.)
- Fiction and nonfiction books about sharks

Take Home Bag for Sharks

Place one or more of the following items in each child's resealable plastic bag. Send the bag home following the introduction or at the end of the unit.

- Picture of Russell to encourage the children to retell the story
- Copy of the "Fun Facts to Share" and a shark sticker
- Photocopies of pictures of the Interactive Display
- The sandpaper shark (see page 98)

FUN FACTS to Share

shark

About Its Body
- The shark has cartilage instead of bones.
- A shark's skin is covered with teeth-like projections, called denticles, instead of scales.
- The shark's ears are inside its head and are connected to the outside by tiny openings.
- All sharks have several rows of teeth growing at the same time. As the shark looses teeth, the ones in back move up to take their place. Scientists believe that a shark may loose as many 30,000 teeth during its lifetime.
- Most sharks have five gill slits on each side of their bodies. When a shark breathes, water goes through its mouth, over the gills, and out the gill openings.

Food
- Depending on their size and preference, sharks feed on many things, including stingrays, bony fish, squid, anchovies, shellfish, other sharks, sea lions, and even garbage thrown from ships.

Habitat
- Sharks live in all the oceans except the Antarctic. They are most numerous in warm ocean waters.

Habits
- Some species of sharks are dangerous to humans (about 30 species). However, shark attacks are rare. Worldwide, there are about 100 per year.
- Most sharks must swim in order to breathe, but other sharks can rest at the bottom of the sea.

Activities for Sharks

- Take a field trip to a local aquarium to see live sharks or visit a display at a natural history museum. If possible, invite a shark expert or representative from your local aquarium or zoo to talk to your students about sharks. Make sure to schedule a question and answer period, as children are very interested in sharks and will have lots of questions.

- Watch a video about sharks. Afterwards, encourage the children to draw or paint pictures about sharks and display them.

- Investigate the length of the longest and shortest sharks. To help the children imagine the length of the longest sharks, stretch out the 59-foot (18 m) string from the Display area on the floor. Have your students lay down beside it (feet to head). If more students are needed, ask another group to join the fun. Now stretch out the 6.5-inch (17 cm) string. Have the children choose something in the room that is the same length to place beside it.

- Set up a shark habitat in the water table. As the children learn more about sharks, invite them to make suggestions about things to add to the shark habitat in the Interactive Display area. Ask your group to think about where sharks live and the things they might see as they swim. Students may refer to the books, magazines, and pictures when necessary. As a student offers a suggestion, have him/her place that item in the habitat. Keep the habitat out in your Interactive Display area for continued exploration.

- Make a rough-skin shark model. A shark's skin is covered with tiny, thorny teeth, called denticles, that are made of the same substance as our teeth. If you stroked the skin from back to front, it could cut your hand. Many years ago, their skin was used for sandpaper. To make the model, cut out or trace the picture of the shark on page 100 to make a template. Transfer the picture onto pieces of very course sandpaper. Have each of your students cut out a shark and add an eye, mouth, and gills. Hang the sharks in the Display Area or save them for the Take Home Bags.

- Present an action rhyme for sharks. Repeat the following rhyme. Encourage the students to fill in each blank space with the name of an animal or food that a shark would eat (shrimp, eel, seal, fish, plankton, another shark).

  I saw a shark go swimming by. (*Turn hand side ways and make a swimming motion.*)
  He swallowed a _____. (*Extend hand, thumb underneath, and mimic an eating motion by opening and closing hand.*)
  I don't know why. (*Shrug shoulders, palms up.*)

  Repeat the above rhyme several times, changing the name in the blank each time. For the last verse, finish with, "I know why. 'He was hungry!'")

- Many sharks have names that have been borrowed from other animals or things. Have each student pick a name and then draw a picture to show what the shark may look like. Later display actual pictures of the sharks. Examples to investigate: leopard shark, salmon shark, goblin shark, dagernose, tiger shark, cigar shark, dogfish shark, zebra shark, cookie-cutter shark, bulldog shark, elephant shark, hammerhead shark, seal shark, whale shark, bonnethead shark, crocodile shark, and nurse shark.

- Most bony fish have a swim bladder to help them stay afloat, but sharks do not. They do have a large liver that is packed with oil. Do a simple experiment to show that oil is lighter than water. Fill a clear, covered container half full of water, float some vegetable oil on the top. Secure the top. Pass the container around for each child to see. Encourage the children to shake the container. What happens to the oil?

- Read the book *Rainbow Fish to the Rescue!* by Marcus Pfister (North-South Books, 1995) to the class. Play a version of "flash tag." Make or have each child make a shiny scale out of cardboard covered with foil. Affix a string to the scale to make a necklace. Make a hammerhead shark headband by copying the pattern on page 101 on construction paper. Cut out the shape and attach it to a construction paper strip. Glue the ends of the strip together to form a headband that will fit a child's head. Select one child to be the shark. The shark stands in the middle (wearing the shark headband) while the other "bony fish" line up facing him/her. Have those children wear their shiny "fish scales." When the whistle is blown, the bony fish must run to safety (designate a line on the other side of your play area) while the shark tries to catch them. All the bony fish that have been caught must now give up their scales and become sharks. Continue the game until all the fish have been caught. Repeat as time and interest allow.

- Mark on a world map where sharks live. Read about different kinds of sharks with the children and then mark on a world map the oceans where specific kinds of sharks will migrate. Use light-colored, neon markers to color in the approximate temperature zones of the world's oceans, such as polar, temperate, subtropical, and tropical. See *Informania Sharks* by Christopher Maynard (Candlewick Press, 2000) for additional information.

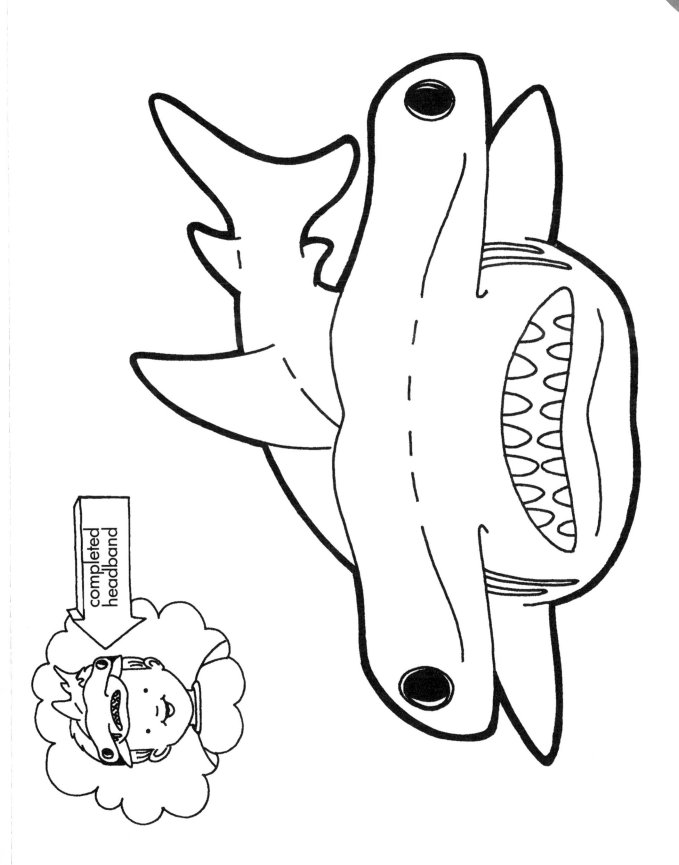

completed headband

Introducing Snakes

Young children seem to have a natural affinity for snakes despite the fact that our culture often portrays them as slimy and dangerous. In reality, the snake's body is smooth and dry. Try to borrow one from a pet store or snake owner and keep it in your classroom for several days. Through observation your students will learn to appreciate this fascinating reptile.

Suggested Visuals

- Picture of Russell
- Full-color pictures of snakes
- A snakeskin
- Plastic or rubber models
- Live snake display

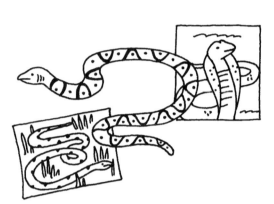

 **Telling the Story**

Gather your students together for a story time. Bring one or more items from the Interactive Display but keep them covered. Hold up the picture of Russell and ask the children what they remember about Russell. Tell this story in your own words.

Yesterday was nice and sunny and Russell and I went for a walk in the woods. Russell, as usual, was excited about walking and he was walking his very fastest walk. Remember how Russell walks? (*Wait to see if they remember before starting a tapping rhythm.*) I walk slowly like this. (*Pat hands on thighs with a slow walking rhythm.*) Russell was way up ahead of me. I wasn't worried because Russell always comes back to me when I whistle like this. (*Whistle and ask the children if they can whistle. Allow those who can to demonstrate their skill.*) Russell had been gone for a while and it was getting late. I was just thinking about whistling for him when I saw him running toward me with something hanging out of his mouth. He dropped it at my feet. I picked it up from the ground and looked at it very carefully. "Wow," I said. "This thing is really strange." It looked like a long tube made of skin. I said, "Hustle, Russell, we need the facts. It is time to go to the library and find out about an animal that leaves its skin behind."

Discuss the Story

Ask the children if they would you like to see what Russell found? Show them a snakeskin. Ask them why a snake would leave his skin behind. If they cannot give an explanation, talk about how a snake sheds its skin when it has outgrown it.

Introduce the pictures and any models that you have collected. Encourage the children to share any information they know about snakes. While the children are examining the materials, share with them some of the interesting facts about snakes from the "Fun Facts" page. If you have a live snake display, show it to the children now and ask for questions. If you do not know the answers, look them up together. Older students will be ready for longer and more detailed explanations and to look up information on their own.

Integrating This Unit

- Study snakes while learning about the rain forest. Set up a rain forest in your classroom. Provide the children with a cave made from a cardboard box. Have the students paint it in the colors of the forest. Hang crepe paper streamers from your ceiling along with some string to which you can attach some homemade snakes, birds, and monkeys. Roll up some brown butcher paper into tubes and tie the tubes at intervals with twine for trees. Make a waterfall out of large unit blocks that have been placed in a staircase configuration and cover them with blue cellophane. Place some rubber models of snakes, lizards, and fish in or near the "water." Ask the students to bring their stuffed toy animals from home to depict animals that would live in the rain forest. Play a recording of rain forest sounds while the children play in the rain forest.

- Set up a "Pet Store" in the dramatic play area. Gather plastic and stuffed animals for exotic and common pets living in the store. Provide books on pets, pet toys, pet food, boxes for animal cages, plastic containers for aquariums and terrariums, and a cash register and play money.

Interactive Display for Snakes

Choose from the following:
- Picture of Russell
- Several pictures and models of various kinds of snakes
- Snakeskin
- Two lengths of rope—a 6 in. (16 cm) length and a 33 ft. (10 m) length to represent the shortest and longest snakes
- Piece of elastic to demonstrate the elasticity of a snake's mouth
- A battery-powered handheld back massager to help demonstrate how snakes "hear"
- Set up a live display.
    1. Garter snakes are easy to keep and are available at most pet shops. Note: Young children should not handle the snakes, as many snakes carry salmonella. Wash hands thoroughly after handling. Clean any surfaces they have touched with a bleach and water solution.
    2. Babies do well in a plastic "Kritter Keeper" or "Reptile Ranch" type housing. Adults can live in a screen-top tank with a tight fitting top. Remember that snakes are masters of escape.
    3. Cover the floor of the tank with paper towels. Fill a pet dish with water. Add two "hide areas" and a "basking area."
    4. An ordinary light bulb in a reflector fixture above the tank will make a good heat source and insure that you see a lot of your snakes. To save power, put the light on a timer.
    5. Snakes are carnivores and eat a variety of amphibians, rodents, and worms. Talk to a pet store owner about "garter grub."
- Fiction and nonfiction books about snakes

Take Home Bag for Snakes

Place one or more of the following items in each child's resealable plastic bag. Send the bag home following the introduction or at the end of the unit.

- Picture of Russell to encourage the children to retell the story
- Copy of "Fun Facts to Share" and a snake sticker
- Photocopies of pictures taken of the Interactive Display
- Photocopies of any pictures taken during the story dramatization
- If possible, a piece of snakeskin

FUN FACTS to Share

snake

About Its Body
- Snakes are reptiles and are covered with dry scales.
- Snakes are cold-blooded and need the sun to keep them warm.
- Snakes do not see very well and have no ears.
- A snake uses its tongue and a special organ on the roof of its mouth to smell.
- Snakes can sense movement around them through vibrations.
- Snakes cannot chew. They swallow the animals that they hunt whole. They unhinge their jaws and spread their elastic mouths wide open.

Food
- Depending on where the snake lives and its size, it may feed on earthworms, insects, small mammals, fish, frogs, lizards, birds, and other snakes.

Habitat
- Snakes live almost everywhere—on land, in trees, underground, in lakes, rivers, and oceans.

Habits
- Some female snakes lay their eggs in a nest and then go away. Others carry the eggs inside their bodies until they hatch.
- Young snakes are ready to hunt soon after birth or hatching.
- Most snakes are shy and avoid being seen.
- Snakes move in a variety of ways. Some move from side to side, pushing their bodies against obstacles to propel themselves forward. Other snakes glide forward in a straight line, raising segments of their bodies off the ground to move forward. Sidewinders coil up in an "S" shape and then throw their bodies sideways, skipping quickly across the hot desert sand.

Activities for Snakes

- Invite someone to talk with the class about snakes and keeping snakes as pets. This is a good way to introduce the unit. (Often the speaker will provide the children with a guest for the classroom.)

- How does a snake hear? If you have a massager, hold it on each child's hand. Ask the children how it feels. Explain that these are vibrations and this is how a snake "hears." What else makes vibrations that we can feel? Demonstrate drums, piano, loud radio, etc. What vibrations would a snake hear?

- Demonstrate the elasticity of a snake's mouth by stretching out a piece of elastic. Measure the elastic when it is stretched out (snake's mouth open/eating) and when it is contracted (snake's mouth closed/not eating). Measure using nonstandard units.

- To help the children get a better understanding of the size of snakes, have them make some paper chains the size and color of their favorite snakes. Hang these snakes around your room. For younger children, use the snap-together cubes that are available in catalogs for early childhood classrooms.

- Snakes vary in size. The reticulated python of Southeast Asia is the longest at up to 33 ft. (10 m). The smallest snake is the thread snake of the Caribbean at 6 in. (15 cm). Have your students measure and cut pieces of yarn or string against the lengths of rope in the Interactive Display (shortest and longest snakes). Store the strings in the Take Home Bags.

- Make play clay snake models. Set play clay on a table in your activity area this week. Encourage the children to make their own snake shapes with the play clay and decorate them with craft materials (buttons, beads, sequins, yarn).

- Talk about the concept of camouflage. Explain camouflage as an animal defense mechanism to your group. If possible, show your students a piece of camouflage clothing that hunters or soldiers use. Ask them to think of other animals that are protected this way, for example, squirrels, turtles, frogs, salamanders, and polar bears.

- Supply each child with some colorful background paper that represents grass, bark, sand, or water. Cut several snake shapes from colored construction paper. Supply a variety of colored stripes, spots, chevron, and diamond shapes. Have the children choose a snake and decorate it to closely match their background paper.

- Make a snake bracelet or pin. Read aloud the book *The Girl Who Wore Snakes* by Angela Johnson (Orchard Books, 1993) to the class. Using molding compound (clay or a compound that you can bake in the oven), each child can make a snake-shaped bracelet or pin.

- If appropriate, share books about poisonous snakes with the children. Show them some pictures of the fangs and explain how they work. Afterward, introduce a syringe (minus the needle) and explain that the invention of the hypodermic needle was based on the fangs of poisonous snakes. Supply the children with syringes (no needles) and a tub of water. Have them practice using the syringes (great for developing fine motor skills). Later have the children make "syringe art" by filling the syringe with paint and squirting the paint onto paper (watercolor paints and paper work the best).

- Read aloud the book *The Greedy Python* by Richard Buckley (Simon and Schuster, 1998) and then have the children act out the story. To make a costume for the python, obtain 5 yards (4.5 m) of green stretchy cloth (latex works well). Sew the ends together to form a long tube. For the other characters cut head-sized strips out of construction paper, staple the ends for a circle and affix ears, eyes, tails, horns, trunks, quills, etc., to represent the other animals in the story. As the narrator reads the story have the "python" lift his/her costume to admit the proper animal. Each will then hold up a section of the python's body. After the python coughs up all the animals, have him/her slowly remove the green material and wad it into a ball to be left on the floor.

- Read aloud the book *A Nice Walk in the Jungle* by Nan Bodsworth (Penguin Putnam, 1992) and then act out the story with your class. Use the python costume from above for the snake. As the narrator reads the story, substitute the names in the book with names of classmates. Finish the play with a herbivore snack (fruits and vegetables) for the participants.

- Perform the following finger play.
    Sunny is a beautiful garter snake. (*Wiggle index finger on opposite palm.*)
    He lives near the shore of a little lake. (*Curl the finger to indicate a snake at rest.*)
    He wiggles and squiggles to catch something to eat, (*Wiggle finger and pounce.*)
    Because, you know, he has no feet! (*Wiggle a finger and then curl it on palm.*)

- Make snake-shaped cookies for snack. Have the children roll small balls of cookie dough into snake shapes, coil, and place them on the cookie sheets. Press to flatten the snake shape slightly. Bake as directed.

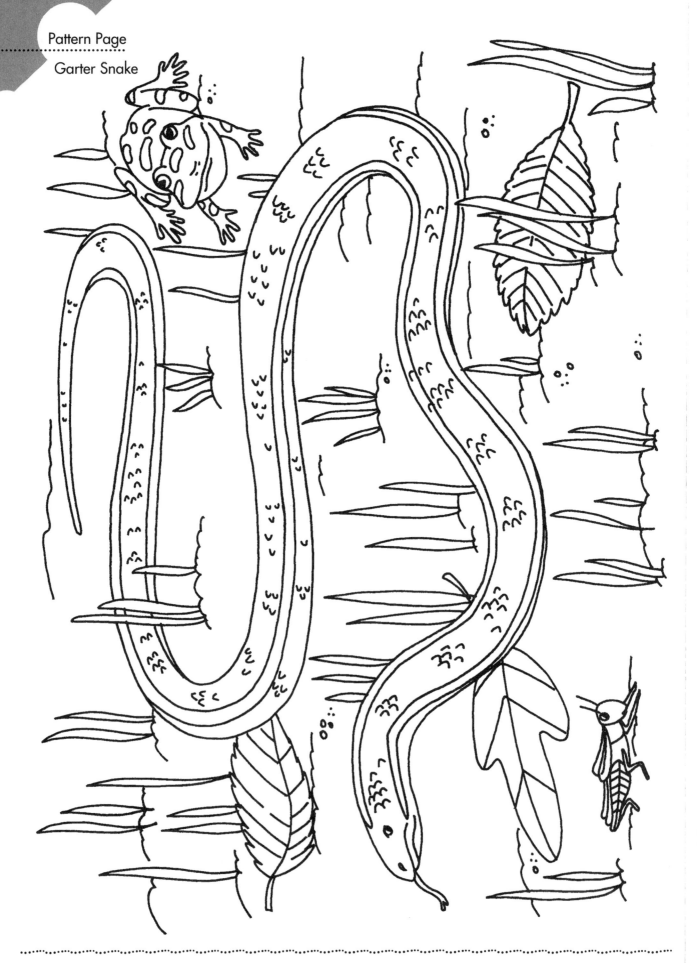

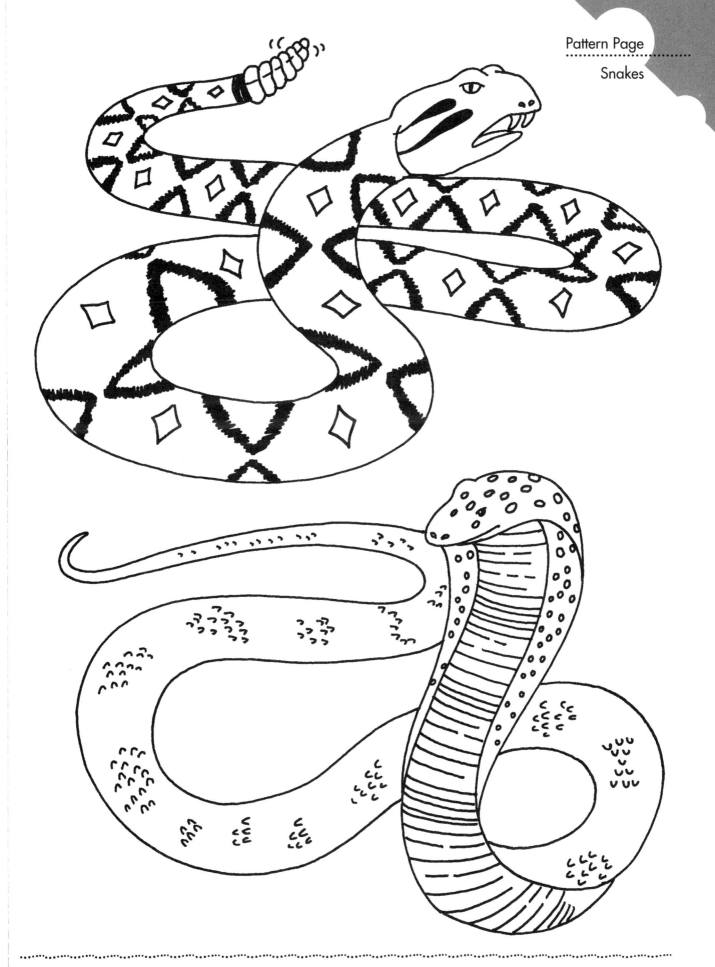

109

Introducing Turtles

Most children have had opportunities to see turtles either at a pet store, nature center, aquarium, or in nature. Turtles with their hard shells for homes, slow pace, and ability to camouflage make ideal animals for children to observe and investigate.

Suggested Visuals

- Picture of Russell
- Full-color pictures of several types of turtles
- A live turtle or a plastic model

 **Telling the Story**

Gather the children together for a story time. Bring one or more items from the Interactive Display but keep them covered. Hold up the picture of Russell and ask the children what they remember about Russell. Tell the following story in your own words.

It had been raining constantly for two days. Poor Russell looked sad. When the weather finally cleared, Russell was eager to go for a walk to the part of the woods near a small pond, his favorite place to investigate. You know how he runs when he's excited, right? (*Have the children demonstrate.*) Well, before I could leave, I had to put on my boots because I knew it was going to be very muddy in the woods. Meanwhile, Russell kept running back and forth, back and forth (*Rock body from side to side.*) until we could leave the house.

Sure enough, it was muddy in the woods, especially around the water. Russell had to slow down a bit (*Tap knees at a slower pace.*) because of the mud. As I walked, my boots kept getting stuck in the mud so I had to take slow, deliberate steps. (*Make slow, exaggerated sounds.*) Soon we reached a wide path that was covered with a thick layer of leaves. We were strolling along that path when Russell saw something that really interested him. Russell kept running around and around it, sniffing and sniffing. I couldn't tell what it was right away, but then I spotted something that looked like a rock with interesting markings. "Come on, Russell," I said, "that's a neat rock, but rocks don't smell."

I started to walk down the path again and Russell trailed behind for a while, looking back at the rock. Then Russell decided to take the lead and headed (*Make a rhythmic patter on knees.*) toward the water. As we stepped close to the water's edge, Russell stopped dead in his tracks! (*Pull body back.*) He took one sniff and jumped way back, blinking his eyes and shaking his head. (*Shake head.*) I tried to see what Russell had found, but I only noticed something very small slip into the water, making the tiniest ripple.

By that time, Russell had bolted back to the path, and I followed him. Right in front of our eyes, the strangest thing happened! Do you remember the rock that Russell had been sniffing and sniffing? Would you believe that it started to move? Really!

I said, "Hustle, Russell, you were right! That wasn't a rock at all. Let's find out about the animal that looks like a rock but has legs and can move!"

Discussing the Story

Ask the children what animal they think this could be? What do they think it was that slipped into the water? Make a list of all the responses. As you pass around pictures of a variety of turtles, share some of the facts about the baby turtles. Explain to the children that the eggs that the hatchlings come from have an odor that dogs don't like! Find out what the children would like to learn about turtles and introduce some of the items from the interactive display. Share some facts about turtles from the "Fun Facts to Share" page.

Integrating This Unit

- Integrate this unit on turtles with a study of pets and their care. If interested, set up a pet shop in the dramatic play area.

- Combine this with a study of amphibious animals.

- Link this with a study of animals and their homes. Have all of the children participate in making a mural where each takes a different animal and represents it in its home.

Interactive Display for Turtles

Choose from the following:
- Picture of Russell
- Full color pictures of different types of turtles
- A live turtle display
- Rubber or plastic models of turtles
- A turtle shell
- Small styrene foam eggs with a crack drawn on each
- Clawed garden tool and a pair of flippers, representing the feet of a pond turtle and a sea turtle
- Tortoise shell items such as hair ornaments, and sunglasses
- Set up a prehistoric display with model dinosaurs, whales, turtles, and cockroaches.
- Create a pond for your display area. Secure a small aquarium or plastic shoebox. Fill the bottom with an inch of mud and then an inch of grave. Add some decayed leaves and a few pond plants. Add pond water and allow your "pond" to sit out of direct sunlight for a few days. Then add more pond water, water insects, snails, and tadpoles. After a time, return the plants and animals to the real pond.
- Fiction and nonfiction books about turtles

Take Home Bag for Turtles

Place one or more of the following items in each child's resealable plastic bag. Send the bag home following the introduction or at the end of the unit.

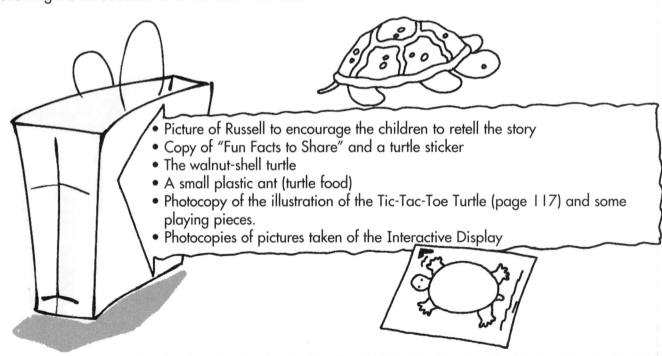

- Picture of Russell to encourage the children to retell the story
- Copy of "Fun Facts to Share" and a turtle sticker
- The walnut-shell turtle
- A small plastic ant (turtle food)
- Photocopy of the illustration of the Tic-Tac-Toe Turtle (page 117) and some playing pieces.
- Photocopies of pictures taken of the Interactive Display

FUN FACTS to Share

turtle

About Its Body
- Turtles who spend time in ponds have clawed feet that make it easy to dig in mud and to tear food.
- Sea turtles have broad, webbed feet that act as flippers.
- The turtle's top shell is called a carapace. The plastron is the name for the bottom shell. The scales on both shells are called scutes and are made of keratin, the same protein substance as human fingernails.
- Turtles have no teeth, but many, including the snapping turtle, have jagged beaks and strong jaws.
- Turtles are reptiles with hard shells that they use for protection.

Food
- Turtles eat a variety of foods. They like all kinds of insects, some plants, many kinds of small fish and fish eggs.

Habitat
- Turtles are found worldwide. They live on land or in the water. Land turtles move slowly with their clubbed feet and high-domed shells.

Habits
- For protection against enemies, many turtles are able to pull their heads and legs into their shells.
- Turtles live much longer than most animals. Some have been known to live 100 years!
- All female turtles lay their clutch of eggs on land—even the giant sea turtles. Mother turtles do not sit on their eggs like birds.
- A newly hatched baby turtle is called a hatchling. As soon as it hatches, the hatchling follows the light to find the water. It is a very dangerous journey because the hatchlings are such easy prey for birds, raccoons, foxes, lizards, and, in the water, large fish.

Activities for Turtles

- Invite a pet shop owner to bring in a several turtles and to talk about their characteristics and suitability as a pet. (Some people have turtles as pets, especially the box turtle and the wood turtle.) Give the children opportunities to observe closely, providing rubber gloves for each child if it is appropriate to touch the turtle. Make a list of qualities that make a turtle a good pet (small, quiet, interesting to watch) versus any drawbacks (inactive, need gloves to touch). If possible, keep the turtle for several days and assign times for the children to observe. Have them tape record their observations. During group time, play the recordings for the class.

- Talk about the classroom pond. Ask the children to list everything that was used to establish the pond. Record the items on a chart. Also include words they used to describe the pond. During group time each day, record any additions and/or changes made to the pond.

- Divide a large piece of paper in half. On one half draw an egg with a small crack in it. On the other half, draw an egg with a red diagonal line through it. Place the paper on a table with several pictures of animals that do not lay eggs and those that do. Encourage the children to sort and place the pictures on the correct half of the paper. Leave this activity out for continued use. After the children have completed the activity several times, have them glue the pictures down and hang the paper in the display area.

- Play a turtle shell and egg guessing game. Split several walnut shells in two. Divide your class into teams of two. Provide each team with three halves of the walnut shells and a small, white egg shape (dried balls of white modeling dough made several days ahead of time). Instruct one of the children on each team to place the egg under one of the turtle shells and slide the shells around rapidly. When they are done sliding the shells, line them up. The other child on the team must guess where the turtle egg is hidden. Make sure each child gets at least one turn. Save several of the games for continued use.

- Make walnut shell turtles. Show the children several colored pictures of various kinds of turtles. Point out the differences and similarities. Use the shells from the turtle and egg game (above). Give a half shell to each child and instruct him to paint the shell in a turtle pattern. Add clay or modeling dough head, feet, and a tail.

- Make turtle costumes from paper grocery bags. Precut the bags for the children. Open the bag completely and then cut down the center of one side until you get to the bottom of the bag, where you will continue to cut, making a large circle for the neck. Cut holes on each side for the arms. Have the children identify the carapace (upper shell) and the plastron (bottom shell) and paint their "shells" accordingly.

- Read Aesop's fable "The Tortoise and the Hare" to your class. Allow the children to help make up a similar story where a very fast animal challenges the very slow turtle to a race. The fast animal (rabbit, cheetah, dog, or horse) will brag about his speed to anyone who will listen. During the race, the fast animal is distracted several times while the turtle moves steadily on to win the race. Have the children take turns playing the fast animal and the turtle while several "turtles" offer advice and cheer their friend on during the race.

- Plan a field trip to a near-by pond to observe pond life or visit your local aquarium or pet shop.

- Make edible "turtles" by dipping walnuts or pecans into melted caramel. Drizzle with melted chocolate.

- Play the game "Tic-Tac-Toe Turtle." Cut turtle shapes out of green construction paper or poster board. Make a tic-tac-toe grid on the turtle shape and laminate (see page 117). Cut several interestingly shaped tic-tac-toe playing pieces out of various shades of green and brown construction paper. Demonstrate how the game is played. When the game is finished, note the interesting patterns that have been created on the "shells."

Introducing Frogs

Frogs are non-threatening to young children. Children often like to catch frogs and bring them home. Frogs go through the stages of their life cycle fairly quickly. Young children will delight in observing and recording the changes that they see and releasing the fully formed frogs back into their natural habitat.

Suggested Visuals

- Picture of Russell
- Full-color pictures of frogs in books
- Rubber/plastic models of frogs or live frogs and tadpoles from a nearby pond

 **Telling the Story**

Gather the children together for a story time. Bring one or more items from the Interactive Display but keep them covered. Hold up the picture of Russell and ask the children what they remember about Russell. Tell the following story in your own words.

Yesterday, Russell and I decided to walk to our favorite pond. Russell is a very curious dog and that sometimes gets him into trouble. (*As you hold up Russell's picture, ask the children what they remember about Russell. Take some time for the children to share some memories of Russell.*)

On the way to the pond, Russell was walking his very fastest walk. (*Begin the quick tapping rhythm.*) He was way up ahead of me because I was walking at a slower pace. (*Tap hands on thighs slowly.*) I knew that Russell would stop and wait for me once he reached the pond. Russell loves it there. There is so much to see at the pond. (*Have the children identify different animals that live on and near a pond.*)

When I arrived, I stood and watched Russell. He was crouched down and it looked as though he was sneaking up on some rocks that were close to the edge of the pond. As he reached the rocks, something leaped off one of them and into the water with a big splash. Russell was so surprised that he lost his balance and tumbled into the water—ker-plunk! I couldn't help but laugh—Russell looked so funny. When I stopped laughing, I said, "Hustle, Russell, we need the facts. It is time to go to the library and find out what kind of an animal surprised you so much that you fell into the water.

Discussing the Story

Ask the children to guess what kind of animal surprised Russell. Make a list of their guesses. Now introduce the pictures, rubber/plastic models, and/or live frogs to the children, saying, "Here is the animal that surprised Russell. What is it?" Encourage the children to share their knowledge of frogs. Ask the children: How do frogs move? What sound do they make? What color are they? What do they eat? Record the children's answers on chart paper. At the end of the unit on frogs, ask these same questions again and record the answers. Did the children answer any of the questions differently?

As the children continue to look at the materials you have collected, share some facts about frogs from the "Fun Facts to Share" page. Ask for questions. If you cannot answer the questions, look up the answers with the children. Older students will be ready for longer and more detailed explanations and to find information on their own.

Integrating This Unit

- Bring some toads into your classroom. Have the children observe them for a day or two. Make charts/pictures that compare and contrast the two species.
- Combine this unit with one on the study of wetlands. Find out how pollutants in the water may cause the frog to become extinct. What are some things that your group could do to help the creatures that live in the wetlands?
- Set up a miniature rain forest in your classroom (see Snakes section) and combine the study of frogs with one on rain forests and animals that live there, such as snakes, bats, insects, and monkeys. If your local zoo has a rain forest section, plan to make a visit.

Interactive Display for Frogs

Choose from the following:
- Picture of Russell
- Full-color pictures of various kinds of frogs
- Rubber and/or plastic models of frogs
- Models depicting the life cycle of frogs (available in science catalogs or borrow from school science department)
- Live display of frogs:

    Collect frogs and/or tadpoles from a local pond. Fill an aquarium or clear plastic container with pond water. Add some rocks for the frogs to sit on. Cover the top of the container with a firm-fitting lid that allows plenty of air through. If it is not possible to have these live creatures in your room, use a clear container, rocks, muddy-looking water, and rubber/plastic animal models and plants to imitate a pond environment. Use some clear marbles as eggs and plastic tadpoles. (There are small creatures that look like tadpoles available in the fishing departments of discount and/or sporting goods stores.) Note: Frogs may carry salmonella. Do not allow young children to touch the frogs. Wash hands thoroughly after handling and clean any surfaces that the frogs have touched with a bleach and water solution.
- Fiction and nonfiction books about frogs

Take Home Bag for Frogs

Place one or more of the following items in each child's resealable plastic bag. Send the bag home following the introduction or at the end of the unit.

- Picture of Russell to encourage the children to retell the story
- Copy of "Fun Facts to Share" and a frog sticker
- Photocopies of pictures taken of the Interactive Display
- Photocopy of pictures taken during story dramatization
- Life Cycle of a Frog puzzle (page 124)
- String used to measure ten lengths of the child's body
- String used to measure the length of the child's leap.

FUN FACTS to Share

frog

About Its Body
- There are about 4,000 types of frogs in the world.
- Frogs are amphibians. They live on land and in water.
- Different types of frogs have different kinds of feet. Some have sticky toes for climbing. Some have pointed toes for digging. Others have webbed feet for swimming.
- A frog needs to stay wet and cool. A frog absorbs water and air through its skin. Its slippery skin also helps it to escape from enemies.
- Many frogs are colored like their background. This camouflage helps frogs hide from their enemies.
- Most frogs begin life as one of a mass of jelly-like eggs. Tadpoles grow inside these eggs until they are big enough to break free into the water. Tadpoles change and grow into frogs.

Food
- Frogs do not hunt their food. They sit and catch insects with their long sticky tongues.

Habitat
- Frogs live almost everywhere on Earth except the arctic regions. They have been on Earth a very long time, even before the dinosaurs.

Habits
- In places that have cold winters, frogs dig holes in the bottom of ponds and lakes and hibernate until spring.
- Most frogs can leap 10 times their body length.
- Each kind of frog makes a certain call to attract a mate.

Activities for Frogs

- Collect frog eggs or catch some tadpoles with the children at a nearby pond or stream. Set up your live display together, using plastic gloves while handling the frogs. If this is not possible, gather the specimens yourself and introduce the eggs/tadpoles at a group time. (If you are unable to have a live display in your room, create an artificial display. Change the display regularly, imitating the frog's life cycle as best you can.) Encourage the children to describe what they see and record their observations with drawings. Show the group a picture/model/diagram of the frog's life cycle and have them predict what will be happening in their live display. Have them look regularly for changes to record. Save the drawings. At the end of the unit, have the children arrange their drawings in order, ending with the picture of releasing the frogs back into their natural environment. Put the pages together to make a classroom book.

- Assemble a frog puzzle. Provide a copy of pattern page 124 for each child. Discuss the picture with the children. Point out the stages of the frog's life cycle. Have the children color the pictures and then cut along the dotted lines. Now they are ready to put the puzzles together. If you like, save the puzzles for the Take Home Bags.

- Perform the following finger play.
    Five green and speckled frogs (*Hold up five fingers.*)
    Sat on a speckled log (*Fingers rest on opposite forearm.*)
    Eating some most delicious bugs. (*Rub your tummy.*)
    One jumped into a pool (*One finger leaps into a pretend pond.*)
    Where it was nice and cool. (*The finger circles the pond.*)
    Then there were four green and speckled frogs. (*Four fingers rest on opposite forearm.*)
    (*Note: Repeat lines until there are no frogs on a log.*)

- Read aloud the book *Jump, Frog, Jump!* by Robert Kalan (William Morrow & Co., 1995). Acquire or make the following props: plastic/paper goldfish, plastic/paper snake, plastic/paper turtle, a net, and a basket. Assign the following parts to the children: frog, fish, snake, child with net, child with basket, and child who sets the frog free. As you read the story aloud again, have the children act out their parts.

- Frogs eat insects and other small animals. Cut out or have the children cut out shapes of several insects/animals that frogs eat such as flies, tadpoles, mosquitoes, smaller frogs, bees, and ants. Cut a large frog tongue shape out of clear adhesive plastic and place it on a table. Have each child come up to the table, tell what the creature is and stick it on the tongue. After everyone has had a turn, cover the tongue with the "frog food" attached with another sheet of clear adhesive plastic. Place the project in the display area.

- Frogs can leap a distance of ten times their body length. Find out how far each child can leap and compare that with ten of his body length. Have each child measure and cut a string that is ten times his body length and one the length of the leap. (Use two different colors and label the strings with masking tape.) Save the strings for the Take Home Bag.

- Make a frog face mask. Copy the frog face pattern (see page 125) onto poster board. Provide styrene foam trays or green construction paper, table tennis balls, or cotton balls for eyes, party favor blowers, and black paint or markers. Trace the frog face on a styrene foam tray or green construction paper for each child. Cut around the face shape and make a slit for the mouth. Have the children paint black pupils on the eyes and glue them on the face. Insert the party favor blower into the slit to become the frog's tongue.

- Listen to and mimic various frog mating calls. The male frog's mating call attracts females and keeps other frogs out of the male's territory. Mating calls vary greatly from species to species. Play a recording of the mating calls. Have the children try to imitate the sounds. Use the following suggestions or think of your own ways to create frog sounds: leopard frog—scratch a wet balloon; spring peeper—make high-pitched, bird like peeps; American bull frog—say "jug-of-rum" over and over again; green frog—pluck a guitar string. After the sounds are perfected, create a "frog band" and perform for another class.

- Compare frogs with toads. Provide pictures so the children can compare the two species. Make a chart about the differences. Some examples include: Frogs—smooth, moist skin; long back legs; long leaps, found in or near water. Toads—dry, lumpy skin; short back legs; short hops; found in woods farther from water.

- Learn about what is happening to frog populations. Frogs are in danger due to problems created by people. Examples include water pollution, pesticides, thinning ozone layer, and construction in the areas where frogs live. Find out what people can do to help. Conduct a search on the Internet for the topic "preservation of wetlands" to learn more information.

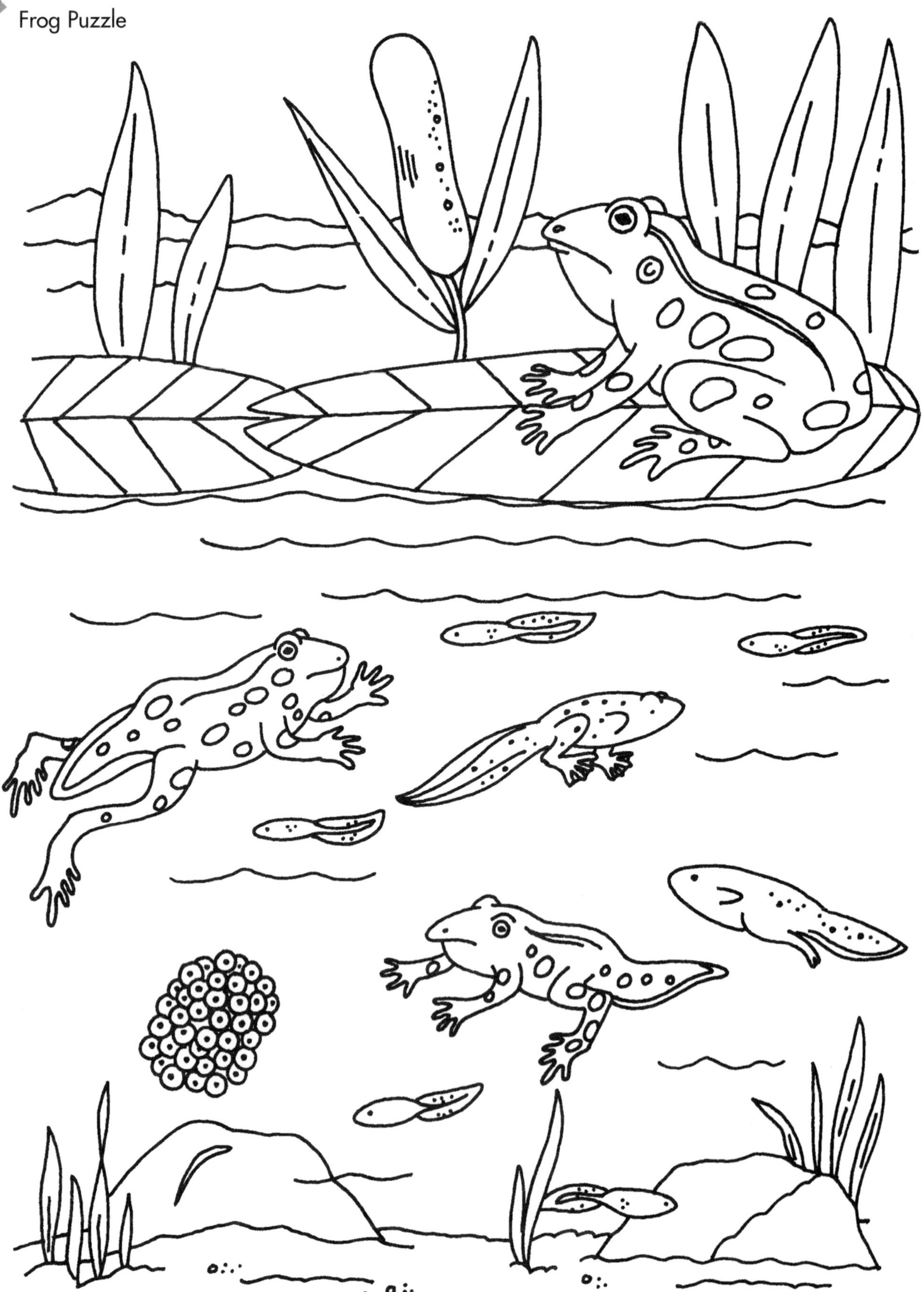

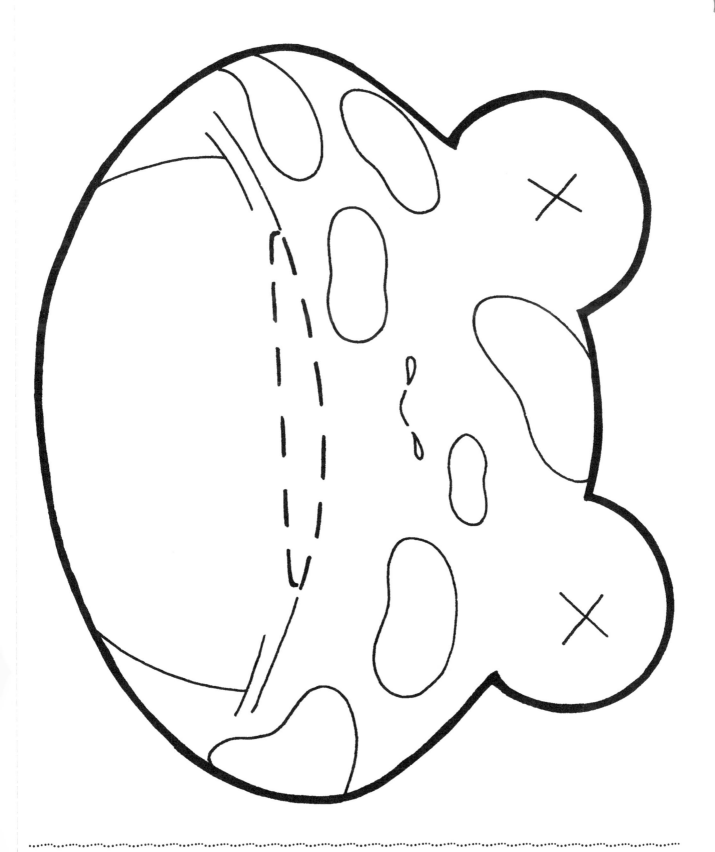

Literature Suggestions

Ants

Berman, Ruth. *Ants*. Lerner Publications, 1996.
Calder, S.J. *If You Were an Ant*. Daniel Weiss Assoc., 1989.
Cameron, Polly. *"I Can't" Said the Ant*. Scholastic, 1963.
Demuth, Patricia Brennan. *Those Amazing Ants*. Macmillan Publishing, 1994.
Dorros, Arthur. *Ant Cities*. Harper Collins Publishers, 1987.

Earthworms

Cole, Henry. *Jack's Garden*. Greenwillow Books, 1995.
Glaser, Linda. *Wonderful Worms*. Millbrook Press, 1992.
Himmelman, John. *An Earthworm's Life*. Children's Press, 2000.
Lemieux, Margo. *Full Worm Moon*. Tambourine Books, 1994.
McLaughlin, Molly. *Earthworms, Dirt, and Rotten Leaves: An Exploration in Ecology*. Atheneum, 1986.
White, Jr., William. *An Earthworm Is Born*. Sterling Publishing Co. Inc., 1975.

Hermit Crabs

Carle, Eric. *A House for Hermit Crab*. Picture Books Studio Ltd., 1987.
Fowler, Allan. *Life in a Tide Pool*. Children's Press, 1996.
McDonald, Megan. *Is This a House for Hermit Crab?* Orchard Books, 1990.
Pledger, Maurice. *By the Seashore*. A. J. Wood, 1960.
Sayre, April Pulley. *Exploring Earth's Biomes: Seashore*. Twenty-first Century Books, 1996.

Monarch Butterflies

Boring, Mel. *Caterpillars, Bugs, and Butterflies*. Northwood Press, 1996.
Carle, Eric. *The Very Hungry Caterpillar*. Philomel Books, 1969.
Herberman, Ethan. *The Great Butterfly Hunt*. Simon and Schuster, 1990.
Hogan, Paula A. *The Life Cycle of the Butterfly*. Raintree Publishers, 1979.
Lasky, Kathryn. *Monarchs*. Harcourt Brace, 1993.

Bats

Appelt, Kathi. *Bats on Parade*. Morrow Junior Books, 1999.
Appelt, Kathi. *The Bat Jamboree*. William Morrow & Co., 1996.
Cannon, Janell. *Stellaluna*. Harcourt Brace, 1993.
Davies, Nicola. *Bat Loves the Night*. Candlewick Press, 2001.
Glaser, Linda. *Beautiful Bats*. Milbrook, 1998.
Milton, Joyce. *Bats*. Putnam Publishing, 1993.
Quackenbush, Robert. *Batbaby Finds Home*. Random Library, 2001.
Shelbar, Sharon and Susan. *Bats*. Franklin Watts, 1990.

Bears

Arnosky, Jim. *Every Autumn Comes the Bear*. G.P, Putnam's Sons, 1996.
Buxton, Jane Heath. *Baby Bears and How They Grow*. National Geographic Society, 1986.
Galdone, Paul. *The Three Bears*. Houghton Mifflin, 1985.
McCloskey, Robert. *Blueberries for Sal*. Penguin Putnam Publishing, 1976.
Merrick, Patrick. *Bears*. Child's World, Inc., 1999.
Pringle, Laurence. *Bearman*. Simon and Schuster, 1991.
Rosen, Michael. *We're Going on a Bear Hunt*. Walker Books, 1989.
Wexo, John Bonnet. *Bears*. Creative Education, 1989.

Skunks

Biel, Timothy. *Skunks and Their Relatives*. Wildlife Education, Ltd., 2000.
Duffy, DeeDee. *Forest Tracks*. The Horn Book, Inc., 1996.
Fair, David. *The Fabulous Four Skunks*. Houghton Mifflin and Co., 1996.
Greenberg, David T. *Skunks!* Little, Brown, & Co., 2001.
Lepthien, Emilie U. *Skunks*. Children's Press, 1993.
Penn, Audrey. *Sassafras*. Child and Family Press, 1995.
Pilkey, Dav. *Big Dog and Little Dog Making a Mistake*. Red Wagon, 1999.
Schleir, Miriam. *What's Wrong with Being a Skunk?* Four Winds Press, 1974.
Swanson, Diane. *Welcome to the World of Skunks*. Whitecap Books, 1999.

Whales

Cole, Joanna. *The Magic School Bus on the Ocean Floor*. Scholastic, Inc., 1992.
Craig, Janet. *Discovering Whales and Dolphins*. Troll Assoc., 1990.
Davies, Nicola. *Big Blue Whale*. Candlewick Press, 1997.
Gibson, Gail. *Whales*. Holiday Press, 1993.
Hayles, Karen, and Charles Fuge. *Whale Is Stuck*. Simon and Schuster, 1993.
Pfister, Marcus. *Rainbow Fish and the Big Blue Whale*. North South Books, 1998.
Shelton, Dyan. *The Whales Song*. Viking Penguin, 1997.

Owls

Arnosky, Jim. *All About Owls*. Scholastic, Inc., 1995.
Benson, Patrick. *Owl Babies*. Candlewick Press, 1992.
Biel, Timothy Levi. *Zoobooks: Owls*. Wildlife Education, Ltd., 1992.
Crebbin, June. *Fly by Night*. Candlewick Press, 1993.
Flower, Phyllis. *Barn Owl*. Weekly Reader, 1978.
Funazaki, Yasuk. *Baby Owl*. Kaisei-sha, 1979.
Roney, Helen. *The Book of North American Owls*. Houghton Mifflin, 1998.
Shedd, Warner. *Owls Aren't Wise and Bats Aren't Blind*. Harmony House, 2000.
Tomlinson, Jill. *The Owl Who Was Afraid of the Dark*. Candlewick Press, 2001.

Penguins

Faulkner, Keith. *The Puzzled Penguin*. Millbrook Press, 1999.
Fowler, Allan. *These Birds Can't Fly*. Children's Press, 1998.
Gibbons, Gail. *Penguins*. Holiday House, 1999.
Kellogg, Steven. *A Penguin Pup for Pinkerton*. Dial Books, 2001.
Lester, Helen. *Tacky the Penguin*. Houghton Mifflin, 1990.
Markert, Jenny. *Penguins*. The Children's World, 1999.
Pfister, Marcus. *Penguin Pete*. North South Books, 1997.
Reid, Keith. *Penguin*. Raintree Steck-Vaughn Publishers, 2001.

Salmon

Cole, Joanna. *The Magic School Bus Goes Upstream*. Scholastic, 1997.
Cone, Molly. *Come Back, Salmon*. Sierra Club Books for Kids, 1992.
Ehlert, Lois. *Fish Eyes*. Harcourt Brace and Co., 1990.
Fegley, Thomas D. *The World of Freshwater Fish*. Dodd, Mead and Company, 1978.
Holling, Clancy. *Paddle-to-the-Sea*. Houghton Mifflin Company, 1941.
Zim, Herbert S., and Hurst H. Shoemaker. *Golden Books Fishes*. Golden Books Publishing, 1987.

Sharks

Arnold, Carolin. *Watch Out for Sharks*. Clarion Books, 1991.
Daly, Kathleen N. *The Golden Book of Sharks and Whales*. Western Publishing, 1989.
Markle, Sandra. *Outside and Inside Sharks*. Aladdin Paperbacks, 1999.
Maynard, Christopher. *Informania Sharks*. Candlewick Press, 2000.
Pfister, Marcus. *Rainbow Fish to the Rescue!* North-South Books, 1995.

Snakes

Baker, Keith. *Hide and Snake*. Voyager Books Harcourt Brace and Co., 1991.
Bodsworth, Nan. *A Nice Walk in the Jungle*. Penguin Putnam, 1992.
Buckley, Richard. *The Greedy Python*. Simon and Schuster, 1998.
Demuth, Patricia. *Snakes*. Grosset and Dunlap, 1993.
Johnson, Angela. *The Girl Who Wore Snakes*. Orchard Books, 1993.
Lauber, Patricia. *Snakes Are Hunters*. HarperCollins, 1988.
Lavies, Bianca. *A Gathering of Garter Snakes*. Dutton Children's Books, 1993.
Linley, Mike. *The Snake in the Grass*. Gareth Stevens Children's Books, 1990.
Linley, Mike. *Weird and Wonderful Snakes*. Thomson Learning, 1993.

Turtles

Arnosky, Jim. *All About Turtles*. Scholastic, 2000.
Cain, Sherida. *Little Turtle*. Crocodile Books, 2000.
Dodd, Lynley. *The Smallest Turtle*. Gareth Stevens, 2000.
Falwell, Cathryn. *Turtle Splash*. Greenwillow, 2001.
George, William T. *Box Turtle at Long Pond*. Greenwillow, 1989.
Gibson, Gail. *Sea Turtles*. Holiday House, 1998.
Schafer, Susan. *Turtles (Perfect Pets)*. Marshall Cavendish Corp., 1999.
Walters, John F. *Hatchlings*. Walker Publishing Co., 1979.
Wildsmith, Brian. *The Hare and the Tortoise*. Oxford University Press, 2000.

Frogs

Flemming, Denise. *In the Small, Small Pond*. Henry Holt and Co., 1993.
Gibbons, Gail. *Frogs*. Holiday House, Inc., 1993.
Glaser, Linda. *Fabulous Frogs*. Millbrook Press, 2000.
Kalan, Robert. *Jump, Frog, Jump!* William Morrow & Co., 1995.
Lionni, Leo. *An Extraordinary Egg*. Randon House, 1998.
Owen, Oliver S. *Tadpole to Frog*. Harper Trophy, 1994.

Russell the Dog